Change in Marriage

A collection of papers presented at the
National Marriage Guidance Council study days

Acknowledgements

The quotation from Laurie Lee's *The First Born* on page 33 appears by kind permission of The Hogarth Press.

Copyright © The National Marriage Guidance Council, 1982.

Published by the National Marriage Guidance Council, Herbert Gray College, Little Church Street, Rugby, Warwickshire CV21 3AP.
Typeset and printed by Dalkeith Press Limited, Kettering, Northamptonshire.

Compiled by Catherine Guy
Edited by Stephen Saunders

ISBN 0 85351 056 3

Contents

Foreword

These are the collected papers of six study days held in different parts of the country in the summer of 1982. The linking theme was 'Change in Marriage'. Each study day focused separately on particular aspects of modern marriage.

The study days attracted a wide range of practitioners working in varying disciplines both with married couples and with those preparing for marriage. The speakers were academics researching into aspects of family life, experienced therapists, and administrators. The study days thus succeeded in bringing together practitioners, trainers and researchers, furthering their communication and mutual understanding.

In 1979, *Marriage Matters,* the Home Office/DHSS working party consultative document, was produced. It called on marriage counsellors to adopt a more research-minded approach to their counselling and education work. Accordingly the National Marriage Guidance Council encouraged its marriage guidance councils to undertake studies into contemporary marriage in their own localities. Many of them responded to this invitation, either through client studies done in co-operation with their colleagues, or by seeking information from the general public. The stimulus of this year of studies by marriage guidance councils encouraged the National Marriage Guidance Council to involve a wider audience in this thinking by arranging the study days, proceedings of which are recorded in this publication.

These study days are a step forward in 'the collaboration between agencies undertaking marital work' which was advocated by *Marriage Matters.* They have brought together a great deal of current information and insight about marriage in this country today. Moreover, they point several ways forward for research and practice in the crucial relationships at the heart of contemporary family life.

Nicholas Tyndall
Chief Officer, National Marriage Guidance Council

Birmingham, 23 April 1982:

Expectations and Outcomes—Bridging the Gap

Chairman *Professor E J Griew, MA, LLB,* Law Department, University of Leicester. Former Executive Chairman, the National Marriage Guidance Council.

Speakers *Penny Mansfield, BSc,* Senior Research Officer, UK Marriage Research Centre. In 1979 completed the first stage of field work on a study of the patterns and processes of early marriage involving 68 couples under 30. The material is being analysed and prepared for publication as a book. It is intended to return to interview the couples again in 1982-83.

Robert Morley, BA, Director, Family Welfare Association. Formerly worked at the Institute of Marital Studies, in the Probation Service and also designed a course in social work at the Hatfield Polytechnic. He is a trained psychotherapist with particular interest in marital work.

Introduction

As the chairman, Professor Edward Griew, pointed out, there are three assumptions implicit in the title 'Bridging the Gap'.

1 That there is indeed a gap between people's expectations of marriage and the reality which ensues.

2 That it can be helpful to understand what discrepancies there may be.

3 That we can try to change the situation by affecting expectations or experience, or by helping people to live with the differences.

The two main speakers approached the subject from different perspectives. Penny Mansfield spoke about the results of research carried out on newly-wed couples for the UK Marriage Research Centre. Robert Morley's paper was based on his long experience in clinical work.

Penny Mansfield

A Portrait of Contemporary Marriage: Equal Partners or Just Good Companions?

'It might be the marriage of the century but there is little equality about it', ran a headline in *The Guardian* last year. Not a reference to *that* wedding in July, but a comment by *The Guardian's* financial editor on the merger between those two arbiters of modern family lifestyle—the retail groups Mothercare and Habitat.

I refer to it here to show that you don't have to wade through lengthy reports by marriage experts to pick up this notion that modern marriage is a union of equals who share the work of caring for the home, each other and the children.

But is this the kind of marriage which men and women getting married in the 80s expect to experience? And perhaps more to the point, is it the kind of marriage they do experience?

Before I describe some of the early findings of a study of newlyweds being conducted at the UK Marriage Research Centre, I would like to reflect briefly on what we mean by 'expectation'.

Last night someone from the BBC rang me to enquire about my contribution to the study day, and he asked: 'Are people's expectations of marriage too high? Of course it depends on what one uses as a yardstick. One man's expectation may be another man's aspiration and one woman's dream. Perhaps one of the most significant changes in marriage is that we reflect at all on what we expect from marriage.

Those of you who spend a lot of your time listening to men and women account for the breakdown of their relationships are probably very familiar with such phrases as 'he didn't live up to my expectations' or 'I expected too much from marriage'. These ascribed causes of marital breakdown would have been unacceptable 50 years ago when the emphasis was on what was expected of you, not what you expected from marriage.

In those days it was a matter of embracing the roles of husband and wife— roles which were carefully defined within our culture. A husband was essentially a provider, a wife a housewife and mother. Provided that each performed his or her role adequately, that was, by definition, a 'good

5

marriage'. That husbands and wives should like each other and be good companions was a bonus; not a requirement. As men and women inhabited different worlds, lack of companionship between spouses wasn't regarded as a legitimate source of discontent. In choosing a spouse it was important to assess his or her potential for performing the husband or wife role adequately. That is why love matches were regarded with such suspicion, for capricious liaisons were intrinsically unstable and stability was what it was all about. Expectations about marriage were socially defined, not individually interpreted.

All this is reflected in Geoffrey Gorer's surveys. In 1950 he found that husbands and wives stressed the importance of being efficient in carrying out their respective roles as breadwinner and housewife. By the time he repeated his survey in 1970 couples were saying that the most important aspect of marriage was that husbands and wives should like each other.

At the Marriage Research Centre, we interviewed 68 couples who were all under 30 years of age on their wedding day and marrying for the first time in 1979. Our study is an exploratory study of the patterns and processes of early marriage, and so we are interested in these couple's expectations of marriage. Originally, we conducted a pilot study in which we asked couples who were about to marry 'what do you expect marriage will be like?' followed by a number of probes designed to focus their attention on many different areas of married life—for example, housework, quarrelling, management of conflict, the sexual relationship. Responses ranged from blank expressions accompanied by 'I don't know' to global aspirations such as 'just to be happy', 'to have a healthy family'. It became clear that these young men and women found it very difficult to articulate their expectations. We assumed this was because they were having to do so from a position of not being married. However, when we came to do the main research with couples who had been married three or four months at the time of the interview we found the answers were equally hackneyed. It was only within the context of the whole interview that expectations became discernible. Alexander Pope's remark to John Gay, 'Blessed is he who expects nothing for he shall never be disappointed', provided a useful clue as the expression of disappointment was often the key to unlocking newlyweds' expectations. Disappointment indicates unfulfilled expectation.

> For example, one wife described how she and her husband had agreed to share the household chores and all seemed to be working well until the wife had to revise for exams: 'Peter was going to take over as I had done when he had been revising but I realised that unless I told him, I organised him, he didn't really do that much. It was a bit of a blow, I really thought we'd got it right.'
>
> And another young wife who described how her husband was 'always out' before they married and now he was out just as much: 'I don't know why I mind so much 'cos I knew it would be like this but I suppose I thought it would be different when we were married and had our own place.'

What Pope did not say (and had he been a member of our research team he might have revised his letter to John Gay) was 'Blessed is he who expects the worst for he may be surprised.'

> This is illustrated by a young husband who described his habit of going drinking after work in the evening and his wife's reaction; 'she don't mind, she's understanding so that was a surprise really . . . something I didn't expect—I thought she'd get the hump.'

So, for some, things were turning out better than expected.

6

A third source of expectations came from comparisons with other marriages and in particular with the marriage they knew best, their parents' marriage. Since role images may be acquired on a casual basis as well as by direct instruction it isn't surprising that children may identify with the husband or wife role through observation of their own parents' behaviour as husbands and wives. In this way many of our respondents gained embryonic notions of marital roles. If the marriage was perceived as successful it was difficult for the son or daughter to say more than 'I'd like to be like them', but some were more specific:

They share everything together. They literally do everything together. They have influenced me a lot because everything they do is together; they never go out separately.

Interestingly, an unhappy marriage was probably more exemplary, but of course by default:

Yeah, I really couldn't have a better insight into what marriage is all about. I've seen the bad side and they are making me wary of what I'm letting myself in for.

Where the marriage had lingered over the final painful stages the son or daughter may have built up an aetiology of a bad marriage. Therefore they had very clear expectations of what not to do:

It's made me think a lot about marriage, what I want from it and what I'm prepared to give. I'm only 21 but I think a lot of people, young people don't give enough thought to it. I've had to think. I know what not to do.

Perhaps the first thing to consider in an enquiry into expectations about marriage is 'why do people get married?' It should be remembered that marriage is still a *rite de passage* in our society—a way of attaining adult status. This was strikingly shown in our study, for apart from those couples who had to spend their early married life living with either set of parents (with unpacked wedding presents standing guard round the marital bed), most brides and grooms left their parents' home for the first time on their wedding day. In this respect getting married (for the first time) marks the end of adolescence and the beginning of adulthood. This comes through vividly in the accounts of the ways in which parental attitudes change after the wedding. Becoming a married man or woman is synonymous with being taken seriously as an adult. Recognition by the parents that the respondent had acquired adult status was evident in the way that the young married couple would be treated as 'guests' and made to feel rather special.

R: My parents—I think they still love me as much as they did but they definitely treat me as a married man. They know Sue comes first now, not them, and it is completely different. They still want to help whenever they can and offer advice, financial support, and everything else—yes my parents treat me like a married man. They sometimes ask my advice now.

I: Do you think your parents treat you any differently now you are married?

R: We get on much better now than we ever did before. We had a sticky patch—my dad he went through one of those middle aged phases, at war with everyone and everything, but since we got married he treats me more as a man in my own right.

I: In what way do they treat you differently?

R: I can't explain it—they seem to—when we go round there or they come round here they seem different—they seem to welcome us differently and treat us like as if we were different people now. Although I'm still their

7

daughter I'm married now, and that seems to make a difference to them. I think it's because I'm away from them so when I see them it's nice, something to look forward to.

As Leonard has suggested, 'spoiling' behaviour on the part of the parents may be part of a mechanism to retain both physical and psychological proximity to the child who has left home, particularly where there are no younger siblings. Another strategy employed by parents of only or youngest daughters was to invite the future son-in-law to live in their home prior to the marriage and to treat him 'like a son'. This strategy was usually very successful when the future husband's relationship with his own family was estranged or where contact was limited because of physical distance.

When asked what they liked about being married, respondents were more likely to refer to 'having a place of my own', 'being free', 'being able to make my own decisions', than they were to comment upon the qualities of their spouses. If, then, many couples expected that marriage would bring with it liberation from parental authority, it seems that their expectations were fulfilled.

Returning to the image of modern marriage as an egalitarian relationship —what evidence is there for such a change? Social scientists attempted to answer this question in the 60s but their findings were confusing and often contradictory. One American sociologist described the emergence of a symmetrical pattern in marriage as a 'bloodless revolution occurring unnoticed in millions of homes'. Later researchers, who were careful to ask what each spouse actually did rather than what they might be prepared to do, agreed that this revolution was indeed unnoticed. It had yet to take place!

But most research does demonstrate the pervasiveness of the ideology of egalitarian marriage. The increasing number of fathers attending births and their greater involvement with the postnatal care of infants led Alice Ross, another American researcher, to suggest that this is a consequence of the establishment of an egalitarian base when both work and jointly maintain their new household during the early months of marriage. So it would seem if we are able to observe marital equality in practice rather than theory we should look at contemporary newlyweds before they become parents.

Turning to our newlyweds, five women were awaiting the birth of their first baby. Three women were unemployed because getting married meant moving but they were seeking new jobs. Sixty wives were working, 54 full-time. So, for most couples, both partners were at work for the same number of hours, both were contributing to the household income and both were as available or unavailable to do the household chores. Over half of the husbands and more than three quarters of the wives believed that spouses should share household chores either by doing everything equally or doing equivalent but different things. But accounts of who does what show wives washing, cleaning and cooking at the end of a day out at work. Doing the shopping, washing-up and making the bed were the chores most likely to be done by men, but very few did more. Men only did the laundry and ironing when their wives were unable to, because of illness.

Middle class men generally did more than working class men, but they were also more likely to believe in marital equality. On the other hand, what working class men did more often coincided with what they said they believed.

Over three quarters of middle class husbands said they believed in marital equality but did little or no housework. Not surprisingly, the husbands' low involvement in traditionally female chores was counterbalanced by their almost exclusive performance of general maintenance tasks such as painting and decorating, cleaning windows, mending simple household equipment. But if one compares these jobs with housework in terms of frequency and repetition can it really be argued that these husbands were participating equally but differently?

Household chores for the most part were not discussed or allocated. They just got done. In spite of the pressure of working full-time outside the home and doing most of the work in the home, few wives expressed dissatisfaction with the status quo. Why? Did they like housework? No, definitely not, most said. There are several explanations:

1 They accept the myth that modern spouses take equal shares as reality. They don't want to confront the discrepancy between what they believe and what actually happens in their own marriages. Despite the repetition of 'I do that' to the catalogue of questions about household activities, wives excused their spouses with remarks such as—'he'd do anything if I asked him'. Or else men were justified for making equal but different contributions. For example:

He's good, does his bit around the home, when I ask him he never refuses or moans. I'm very lucky . . . he's not the sort of man who says 'it's woman's work'.
I know he doesn't do the washing or ironing, but he wouldn't know how so it's better that I do it, but he does do all the decorating and if you'd seen this place when we first moved in you'd realise what a lot of work that involved.

2 Of course so early into the marital routine it must not be forgotten that this was still a honeymoon period when the failure of a partner to live up to expectation or any vague sense of disappointment may have been buried under optimism and the novelty of it all. For example:

I really like doing things myself—it's nice to be able to arrange things as I like and have my own kitchen. I'm enjoying cooking all sorts of different recipes. My mum did everything at home so it's all new for me.

3 As I noted earlier, getting married meant getting a place of one's own and the attainment of freedom. It might not be a dream home but at least you could choose where to put the furniture, when to do the dishes. This first home was like a wendy house; somewhere to play in. Domestic routine was part of this and there was fun and pride in caring for new possessions.

But an overwhelming influence on the attitudes of these new wives was the certain knowledge that they would leave their jobs when they became mothers, probably not returning for several years and then only part-time to fit in with the family's needs. The priority given to the husband's job from the very beginning of marriage was particularly evident from the number of brides who changed their jobs or working hours when they got married. For them paid work came second to domestic responsibilities and the former had to adapt to the latter.

The acceptance of the housewife role at this stage was part of the knowledge that full-time housework is an inevitable corollary of motherhood. So although marriage as an equal partnership is favoured as an ideal, it doesn't appear to be adhered to in the daily agenda of married life for the couples in our study.

So much for equal partners—what about good friends? In the early months before the arrival of children, husbands and wives spend a lot of time together. It was important to most couples to present themselves as a couple. So going out without the spouse was exceptional. The most common outings for men without their wives, were attending an evening class, playing sport and the odd evening or Sunday morning in the pub. Women's outings without their husbands were almost exclusively shopping expeditions with a relative or friend (usually mother) or visits home to mum. Those husbands and wives who, after three or four months of marriage, were spending a lot of time away from home were very clearly failing to live up to their spouses' expectations but it was hoped that they would 'settle down'. The exclusivity of the marital relationship obviously meant less contact with friends with the result that the couple became ever more dependent upon each other for company.

One bride experienced this even on her honeymoon:

> It was strange after all the excitement of the wedding. We got to the hotel and got our room (which was lovely) and we closed the door and we were all alone, just the two of us. We felt, I felt quite lonely. This was it.

Communication was an area where the behaviour of the couples did seem to be living up to expectations. That is, the communication about everyday things. The sharing of more intimate matters was again stressed as important (and the exclusiveness of the spouse as a confidante particularly). However, early indications from the analysis suggest that the desire to 'open up' and have 'heart to heart' talks is more favoured by women. Non-self-disclosing spouses were more often husbands—who didn't see the point of talking about problems and worries.

One husband put it this way:

> Well, I've never been one for that. Can't see the point I mean if something goes badly for you, say the guv'nor gets you down, there's nothing the wife can do. So why talk about it? But now I come in and I'm feeling cheesed off and she's all the time saying 'what is it? what's wrong?' She won't leave me alone.

The ease with which many wives were able to disclose their feelings often inhibited their husbands:

> She always does it before I get my chance to so it always looks a bit soppy if I—she always says she loves me but then if I say I love you as well it just doesn't have the same sort of impact—I mean I do often say I love you but when it really matters—when she's really thinking about it she's already said it so it doesn't—to me in my mind I mean she sort of likes to hear it but in my mind it's lost—it's you know.

I have tried to select a few areas on the agenda of married life to give you some insight into the experience of some contemporary newlyweds. The interviews were far ranging.

To sum up then:

1 Modern marriage may be different to the traditional image of an institution characterised by the absolute authority of the husband and complete submissiveness of the wife, but does that mean it is an egalitarian relationship? The Victorian novel, a major source of our knowledge of social history, abounds with vivid accounts of stern and uncompromising husbands and their obedient and abashed wives. It is this comparison of Mr Barrett of Wimpole Street with the dish-washing, pram-pushing

husbands of the 80s which has justified the belief that contemporary husbands and wives are equal partners. More equal perhaps—but not equal.

2 Furthermore, while at one level we read a lot about the position of women having improved in terms of public equality with recent legislation such as the Equal Pay Act, the Matrimonial Proceedings and Property Act etc. . . . and the growth in the proportion of married women who are working and contributing to the home (now over half, as opposed to one fifth in the 1950s), there seems little evidence for the assumption that this has been accompanied by greater male domesticity.

We must be careful to check the pervasiveness of the ideology of egalitarian marriage. This is how dreams become expectations. And dreams are rarely fulfilled.

The fact that first marriage was for many couples the official end of adolescence was striking. It is an interesting paradox that for these men and women part of the motive for matrimony is to experience independence and freedom. However, in order to achieve that independence they have become involved in a relationship which requires some level of dependence to make it work. I shall finish with the comment of one husband from the pilot stage of the research.

> I like being married, having the home, doing things together. It's what I've always wanted, my own place and, eventually, my own family, but sometimes I feel, well I'm only 22, am I stuck, in a rut maybe? I love Anna, she's a great girl and we do a lot together but I wonder should I have left it later, married later when I'd seen a bit of life, done a few more things. Would I settle better? And then I think, we can do it all together, before the kids come. But she don't want that, and I have to go along with her—give and take I know. But like I say, I'm young, I want to take a bit. But if I hadn't got married, what would I have done in the meantime?

So the spouse who represented a catalyst for liberation has become an inhibitor of freedom after marriage. This is part of the dilemma of 'being separate but together' which Bob Morley will take up.

Robert Morley

Separate but Together— The Essential Dichotomy of Marriage

My starting point for this discussion is different from that of Penny Mansfield, who talked about her research and its findings. I am speaking as a therapist with long experience of working with couples in difficulties with their relationships, as well as with individuals who present themselves for help with their troubles. What I have to say is a consequence of that experience, which has been gathered in a number of different settings, in statutory and voluntary agencies as well as in private practice. Its validity depends upon that experience which has certainly not been systematic in that the people whose work with me is the basis for the conclusions I want to offer you were not selected in a scientific way with reference to their class and social backgrounds or other such factors. They are the random collection of couples and individuals who have presented themselves to a therapist whose work has taken him to a variety of places in the course of 30 years. The concepts I propose to discuss with you are drawn from that experience and should be given as much or as little weight as you think that such a derivation deserves.

For me, these ideas have gained in validity because, through introspection, I find that in various ways the same kind of issues are alive in me. For the true scientist I suppose the inner world is suspect as a source of bias and faulty observation, and while I understand this quite well in respect of human relationships, I find it difficult to believe that what is true in me is not also true in others. Or, to put it another way, what can be observed in others is also true for me. So that, as I have begun to be aware of what issues are being confronted by my patients in their relationships, I feel comforted by the fact that I can also find them in myself and in the important relationships in my life. It takes me away from the image of the therapist as a kind of impersonal object—a view which seems to be more of a caricature than a reality and, when given up, allows me to take in the client's world and test it against my own, and to become aware of and to use my own responses. You will, of course, be able to give what weight you think appropriate to this factor in making your judgements about the validity of my views.

My experience leads me to agree with the view expressed in Paragraph 2.32 of *Marriage Matters*[1]:

> . . . the experience of those who work with marital problems strongly suggests that it is not happiness or its frustration in the simple hedonistic sense that is at issue, but rather what is conceived of as an actual or potential threat to the 'self'. If disillusion and conflict cannot be encompassed without such a threat, or if the anxiety it raises cannot be managed, then an individual risks disturbance in close personal relationships and emotional life.

The concept of the self is not an easy one to define although I suppose we all know what we mean by it. A definition which I find quite helpful is one also quoted in *Marriage Matters,* and drawn from J D Sutherland's *Towards Community Mental Health*[2]. It reads:

> The 'self' is the term we use for the core of personality that preserves continuity in change, and its integrity is what makes change acceptable.

I would add one further aspect to that definition which is that the self may be very strongly influenced by the culture within which it exists and includes components conforming to cultural norms and others conflicting with them. I add this in order to demonstrate that the 'self', although experienced as the core of the personality and thus the most intimate centre of one's existence, is nevertheless connected in quite an important way to the social world. In a sense the social environment is necessary for the self to exist and it is quite difficult to imagine a 'self' in total isolation. Robinson Crusoe took with him to his desert island a lot of social luggage which sustained him and in the end he needed Man Friday. Winnicott has drawn our attention to the fact that for the infant the social environment is bounded by the mother or other intimate caretaker. As he says, you don't see babies, only mothers and babies. The infant self is developed in the interaction with the mother, and without that interaction the infant would certainly not develop and might die psychologically and even physically. The necessity for an intimate other, or others, for psychological as well as physical health remains with us throughout life and the struggle to be with as well as apart from that intimate relationship is perhaps part of the essence of being, and in my view is certainly a fundamental aspect of the marital relationship and other intimate relationships which resemble marriage.

In all the marriages I have worked with this seems to have been a basic problem to which all the others were related, and the struggle of the self both to survive and to develop within an encompassing relationship has usually been paramount. It seems to me that something of this sort lies behind the protest of women which has become crystallised in the modern feminist movement. It is as if many, if not all, women are no longer able to endure the sacrifice of self and the inhibition of self development that traditional roles in marriage have required of them and are drawing attention in a vociferous way to the personal cost of that relationship. Although many of us would consider marriage, or any similar intimate relationship, as potentially developmental, it is well to recognise that it also represents a threat to many people and there is often a fine balance of gains and losses to be negotiated. Importantly, the negotiations have the objective of diminishing anxiety and securing the safety of the self.

In my view these negotiations take place round a number of factors which can perhaps be expressed in terms of pairs of opposite characteristics. In

13

attempting to formulate my ideas in this way I have been very strongly influenced by the work of Erikson, in particular by *Childhood and Society*[3] and especially by his discussion of the phases of emotional growth, each of which he designated by interactive and opposing characteristics. Some of you may remember that his definition of the emotional task for marriage is Intimacy versus Isolation, which has always impressed me as being a graphic definition of what is experienced in intimate relationships. But that definition includes a number of issues which should be separate, and if they are separated they enable us to understand more easily the nature of the anxieties being experienced by each partner, and may help us to learn how the threat to the self is arising.

The first of the factors I want to discuss I call Attachment versus Detachment. Bowlby, in most of his work, has drawn our attention to the importance of attachment, and how relationships are formed and sometimes deformed as a result of the need to attach. He has referred to ethological evidence to provide an understanding of the need for attachment, which he regards as a requirement for survival. Given the helplessness of the infant at birth and for some time afterwards, perhaps few of us would disagree. What I think is underemphasised in Bowlby's work is the ebb and flow of anxiety around the need to be attached which I think goes on through life. He is, of course, aware of it and in one passage quoting the observation of another psychologist, Anderson, he very nicely illustrates in the behaviour of children the fluctuations in levels of anxiety.

> Selecting children estimated to be between 15 months and two and a half years, whose mothers were sitting quietly allowing them to run about in what was presumably a fairly familiar place, Anderson noted the movements of each child relative to the mother over a period of 15 months. Of the 35 children observed, 24 remained throughout within a distance of 200 feet of mother, travelling from her and back again without her taking any action to ensure proximity. Anderson comments on the ability of the children to remain mother-oriented while establishing a distance which takes them out of her immediate control . . . Typically the mother-oriented children moved either directly away from mother or directly towards her, moving in short bursts punctuated constantly by halts. Return towards mother seemed to be accomplished in longer hops and at a faster rate than the outward journey. Halts near mother were infrequent but of relatively long duration; those at a distance were more frequent but much briefer.[4]

I think it may not be too fanciful to suggest that this ebb and flow of mother-orientedness was a consequence of the relative level of anxiety which was having to be managed, and closeness and distance were being balanced to maintain a sense of ontological security. The same management of anxiety is experienced by adults in their relationships with each other and the fluctuation of feeling is, I think, well expressed by the poet Meredith[5] in the following lines:

> With thee the wind and sky are fair,
> But parted, both are strange and dark;
> And treacherous the quiet air
> That holds me singing like a lark.

Just as the infant is looking for the secure distance from mother which enables him to be free enough to pursue his own interests while not being too distant to expose him to overwhelming anxiety, so the adult is endeavouring to find the position between the extremes of attachment and detachment which facilitate the capacity to explore the world freely but yet ensure that a secure base exists from which succour and relief may be gained when the world becomes overwhelming. The position in this spectrum which may be reached by any couple is not usually achieved once and for all and is subject to change during the course of a relationship. It may be that as an individual feels stronger in respect of the world, then the need for attachment will be less great, but if for any reason the world seems overpowering or frightening, then the importance of the attachment may become greater. The rising executive or politician, for example, may feel sufficiently powerful vis à vis the environment to be able to venture further and further away from a basic relationship and to be operating in a very detached way. But should that confidence be threatened, say by redundancy or by illness or any other misfortune, the need for a secure attachment which can be relied upon becomes paramount.

The capacity for attachment, or, to put it another way, the degree of anxiety aroused by the process of attachment, derives from the kind of experiences that an individual has had in the process of growing up. Attachment to parents may have been very gratifying, giving the growing child a feeling of reliability and security fostering growth to maturity. Such a person is likely to make easy, secure attachments which will continue to gratify both partners. On the other hand, attachments may have been insecure and unreliable, giving rise to what Bowlby calls anxious attachment, an excessive fear at being away from the attachment figure and an excessive degree of dependence. Some, of course, are rendered by their experiences as children quite unable to make attachments at all, and their relationships may be characterised by attempts to gain gratification, without regard to the needs of their partners, or by a withdrawal into isolation. For all except the most profoundly damaged, the legacy of childhood is not, however, the last word, and in respect of the spectrum of attachment/detachment individuals continue to strive to find their most comfortable, anxiety-free position on it, and often may be attempting to modify the remnants of the past so that they can live in a more satisfying way.

The second element of relationships I call Commitment versus Disengagement, and it refers to their extension in time, as well as to concepts of exclusivity and promiscuity. Once again what is determining is the degree of anxiety experienced about the continuation of the relationship with one another through time. The level of anxiety generated by the perception of a commitment to an enduring relationship may determine whether the partners can continue with a committed relationship or whether they feel compelled to form promiscuous relationships. It is rather difficult to think of relationships without there being some element of endurance involved, but on reflection it seems possible to regard some very brief encounters as relationships, particularly where they may involve some very intense and intimate interactions. For example, encounter groups may not involve more than a very time limited commitment but nevertheless intense interactions are likely to occur which are also to be found in other relationships. In our society, however, the ideal is the long term, enduring committed relationship having behind it the force of both religion and the law. We have, in fact, almost forgotten that it is an ideal, and until recently, when different ways of relating began to obtrude more publicly, we regarded that as the norm with all the others being thought of as deviant.

Nevertheless it is possible to observe within the traditional arrangement quite striking differences in the way commitment is managed. There are couples who have affairs with other partners either secretly or more openly, and in this way they may perhaps be trying to deal with anxiety about committedness and exclusivity. What is known as open marriage, for example, very specifically abjures the notion of exclusivity, but for those who engage in it this may be the very factor which allows the continuance of a longer term commitment. Similarly the concept of swinging abandons the notion of sexual exclusiveness in favour of promiscuity which enables the relationship to continue while reasserting the freedom to continue to chose.

Robert Weiss[6] in his paper *Couple Relationships* illustrates very neatly the way in which anxiety about commitment is managed in what he describes as 'going together' relationships. He says:

> Couples seem to have a number of rather different kinds of reasons for choosing to 'go together' rather than to live together. Firstly, the couple, perhaps especially the woman, were often unwilling to make public the sexual nature of the relationship. As long as separate residences were maintained, the man did not evidently stay overnight, and there was no pregnancy, those of our respondents were able to maintain a position of *honi soit qui mal y pense*. They could consider their respectability to continue essentially undamaged, whatever others might think. Secondly, either the man or the woman or both were unwilling to become deeply enmeshed in their relationships, despite their attachment, either because they feared that it would end sooner or later, or because they felt it was somehow inappropriate or undesirable and so should end.

Here Weiss is clearly referring to the concept of commitment and the time factor involved and the anxiety which has to be managed. He continues:

> The third kind of reason had to do with the desire of the woman, especially, to retain independence in the management of her affairs and of the man, especially, to retain autonomy and a limit to responsibility. One woman described going together as a most desirable relationship just because it would provide attachment without the problems of shared routines and living arrangements.

The retention of independence and autonomy, the freedom from the restriction of shared routines and living arrangements, are ways of ensuring a freedom from anxiety and the maintenance of a sense of ontological security which might otherwise be threatened by a more deeply committed relationship extending in time, and the limits of the 'going together' relationship is the price which may have to be paid for this sense of security.

It is possible to see this conflict between commitment and disengagement most sharply in a problem which will be very familiar to all those who are engaged in any form of marital counselling. It is the difficulty presented by some couples who may have lived together for several years in reasonable harmony and then they decide to formalise their relationship and get married. Almost immediately their previously harmonious relationship becomes difficult and they find themselves at odds with each other, often to the point of separation and divorce. The problem was one which interested the late Henry Dicks, whose explanation of it was couched in terms of divergence from and conformity to parental models of marriage. I have no doubt that there is something in this, but as I have reflected about the issues involved, the more convinced I have become that at the point of marriage and the formalisation of the relationship into a bond or contract, what has occurred is that the ontological security of either or both of the partners has become threatened by the change in the form of the relationship. Far from increasing the security of the couple, it seems to have undermined it as the anxiety of one or both increases. Often the marriage has taken place not at the wish of the partners but as a result of pressure brought to bear upon them by relatives, notably parents.

Mr and Mrs Adams were an example of this. They had known each other at university, and when they left they began work in the same town, although it had not been a specific choice that they should be together.

Mrs Adams found herself feeling anxious about being away from the community of young people, including Mr Adams, with whom she had shared the previous four years. She and Mr Adams began to see each other, and although they maintained separate flats, spent most of the week with each other in one or other of their flats. This rather informal relationship worked quite well and they were able to enjoy a good sexual relationship with each other.

As time went by, however, they felt themselves more and more pressed by their parents to formalise their relationship and get married. For some time they resisted but found it increasingly difficult to do, and eventually gave in and decided to have a very formal wedding with all the trimmings, while at the same time they maintained inside themselves a feeling of rebellion. However, no sooner had they become formally engaged than they experienced an almost immediate deterioration in their sexual relationship, and this continued up to and after the wedding until their sexual relationship ceased altogether. Despite their shared inner attitude to the wedding and to marriage, they were profoundly affected by its implications in terms of the partnership and their committedness to it. It was especially easy to see in Mrs Adams the conflict between her need to be committed and her anxiety about what it meant in terms of her continued survival as a separate person. For both there was a need not to be identified with other couples who were conventionally married, and it represented a threat to an important sense of themselves if they found themselves behaving like conventional partners.

In general I suspect, although it is no more than a hunch, that it is the feeling of commitment from which there is no escape that gives many couples these days the greatest difficulty with each other. In the past, what was popularly known as the seven-year itch was a manifestation of the same thing, and it is evident that the unremitting nature of the relationship was too much for some couples, who then needed to seek some way of escape from it.

The third element which I want to discuss is the conflict between Intimacy and Alienation. In the impact upon the self and its survival I think that this is the factor which is the most powerful. The concept of self suggests a deep sense of inviolability and kind of inner core of privacy which is safe from intrusion and whose continued existence is secure. The notion of intimacy runs quite contrary to this, however, and suggests a voluntary surrendering of privacy in favour of a profound sense of closeness with another. It includes both physical and emotional closeness and the characteristic of sexual intercourse of one person being inside another is also a feature of the emotional relationship. Intimacy may have at its root the desire to be one rather than two, and in a sense may be a reverberation of the feeling of the foetus in the womb. Such closeness may be very comforting but there can be little doubt that for many it will also be disquieting. At its best intimacy in adulthood contains the joy of feeling understood and accepted by another, of being known within the private depths of the self, and of being able to disclose the deepest, most intimate thoughts to the other without fear of annihilation or mortification. It involves the exposure of vulnerability and weakness in trust and with relief of apprehension and it includes the feeling of tenderness towards the partner and the experience of being cherished by the partner. As is often the case this sense is most easily expressed in poetry, and the following fragment of Auden expresses what I have in mind[7]:

> Souls and bodies have no bounds
> To lovers as they lie upon
> Her tolerant enchanted slope
> In their ordinary swoon . . .

In a sense this is the ideal which few achieve, except perhaps in the first flush of love, and it may be profoundly frightening to those whose sense of identity and selfhood is less than securely held. The penetrating proximity of the other threatens to dissolve the uncertain and insecure boundaries of the self, merging them within the boundaries of the partner. It may be that there is some basic gender difference in this experience as between men and women. Men seem to fear the possibility of being incorporated or engulfed by the other or, on a slightly less frightening level, as in danger of losing a vital part of themselves. Women, on the other hand, seem to fear being split open or of being flooded and deluged by the messiness of the other. For both, the apprehensions are of losing essential aspects of the self and that recovery may not be possible.

In this aspect of relationships it is possible to see most clearly the struggle which feminists have described as political, the attempt as they see it to wield the power in the relationship and to control the other. I think they are right to see this as an important conflict but I would see it rather as a struggle for survival rather than as a struggle for power, and the wish to control is perhaps an expression of the fear of the threat presented by intimacy to the survival of the self. Essentially it is an internal struggle which becomes externalised in the relationship. That is to say, each individual is engaged in a life-long internal conflict between the wish to be close to, even merged with, an intimate other, and the wish to remain separate and apart. In the relationship the wish to be close to another can be easily translated into an anxiety about that other's overwhelming pressure for closeness which has to be warded off.

The problem presented by a couple I will call the Pereiras illustrates this issue quite neatly. Mr Pereira had been brought up in a culture in which men and women had very segregated roles and from a very early age boys were separated from the girls and women and joined the men. There was ample evidence that Mr Pereira found this a very arid situation and experienced the loss of intimacy with his mother as devastating. He did his best in adulthood to get away from that culture and into one in which much closer contacts between the sexes were possible. He married a very warm emotional woman who certainly offered him the intimacy which he craved. In contrast to the rather carefully controlled person that he was, she was almost chaotic and very

18

outgoing in a way which he found very threatening to the extent that he felt that he was not in control in the relationship and could not survive in the flood of feeling which his intense desire for intimacy unleashed. He began to try and retreat from this deluge and to attempt to withdraw into some of the isolation and segregation with which he was more familiar. He complained that she would not respect the boundary between them and that there was no part of the house which was sacrosanct. She invaded it all and could not be kept to the woman's part of it. She even demanded sexual intercourse and would not wait until he felt it was right to initiate sex between them. By the time I saw him it was difficult to get him to acknowledge his own wish for intimacy, and by then he was so anxious that he was retreating to the alienation end of the spectrum in an attempt to control all this anarchic emotion which so frightened him.

The final aspect of relationships with which I am concerned I call Similarity versus Difference. I first became aware of this when I was attempting to understand something about couples who had married inter-racially. What was so striking about many of them was the marked difference between them, and often their problems seemed to be about difference—difference in past experience, difference in expectations and difference in behaviour. Often the differences were so considerable that they seemed to frustrate the objectives of a close relationship, particularly the goals of intimacy, which at some level requires a capacity to identify with the other. At the same time I was aware that difference could often be sexually exciting and that strangeness was often erotic, so that the choice might be one which allowed for the possibility of obtaining erotic pleasures while at the same time blocking others. I also became aware of the safety which the perceived difference brought to those whose own sense of identity was poorly developed or defective. It was as if the threat presented to the survival of the self might be dealt with by the choice of another with whom it was impossible to identify and hence the boundary between the couple would always be in place. Thinking about these questions demonstrated that those who married inter-racially were only at one extreme of possible choices of similarity and difference and that the other extreme consisted of those whose relationships demonstrated a narcissistic choice of somebody who was almost identical.

However, the dimension of similarity and difference encompasses considerably more than the differences of race or culture. Perhaps the most important of these differences is that between male and female, and it is at once possible to see a range of choices extending from confident heterosexual partnerships, through those who choose partners of both sexes, to those who choose partners of the same sex, and to those who can have no partner at all and can only obtain auto-erotic gratification. These choices seem to depend upon the level of anxiety aroused by the perception of sexual difference. Probably none of us is entirely free from anxiety in this respect and attraction always has to overcome it to a greater or lesser degree. For many, perhaps most, this is possible, and a heterosexual choice of partner can be made more or less comfortably. Homosexuals, however, often demonstrate an overwhelming anxiety about the genitals of the other sex to the extent that they are unable to contemplate a sexual relationship with a partner of the opposite sex. Others may assuage the anxiety aroused by the perception of genital difference by choosing partners sometimes of the same sex and sometimes not.

19

It is as if confidence is regained with the same sex partners which allows a subsequent choice of an opposite sex partner, although the confidence so obtained is not enduring and requires continual reinforcement.

The four elements which I have been discussing all involve a conflict in themselves, but the matter is even more complicated than this because each of them may be in conflict with each other. I have already drawn attention to the way in which the desire for intimacy may come into conflict with fears about similarity and thus push the individual concerned in the direction of alienation in order to find a partner whose difference is great enough to assuage those anxieties. Equally, anxieties about commitment and their resolution by an approach towards disengagement may arouse fears about a loss of attachment; and intimacy may only be possible at the expense of commitment, that is to say an intense relationship may only be enjoyed with a partner who would be unlikely to demand a long-term relationship, or with whom the contact was only intermittent. A number of marriages seem to be arranged on that basis with the partners spending quite large proportions of their time away from each other. Some kinds of employment seem to be especially suited to those whose relationships need this kind of interruption in order to keep anxiety at a containable level. Long distance lorry drivers, aircrew on long haul flights, sailors, business executives in international companies and politicians all have opportunities provided by their employment to diminish anxieties aroused by any of the factors I have referred to, and needless to say their wives are provided with the same opportunity. For both parties the terms of their employment may provide them with an admirable way to deal with the difficulties created by their relationship.

What conclusions about marriage should be drawn from this analysis of some of the underlying factors in forming and sustaining a relationship? The first seems to me to be almost self-evident although perhaps it is not. It is that relationships are very complex matters in which the partners are attempting to find a comfortable position for themselves, in which the fears aroused by the presence of the intimate other are at a minimum and the gratifications are at a maximum. For each couple their resolution of the various conflicts will be unique and may include the capacity to be married to each other, or it might not. For others it may not be possible for them to sustain anything like the relationship we have in mind when we talk about marriage. It may be that we should bear in mind that the lifelong relationship of one person with another is only one of the ways in which people form partnerships, and it may not be possible for many people to cope with that way of being together. The sometimes alarming way that statistics about marriage breakdown are presented may be interpreted to suggest that this may be so and that many fewer people than is commonly believed can sustain a lifelong committed relationship.

The second conclusion which I draw follows from this and it is that we should cease to make illegitimate many of the ways in which people can form a relationship. We may have our own private preferences but we should cease to use these preferences as a way of stigmatising the different kinds of arrangements that others make in consequence of their mutual need to diminish their anxieties in order to enable life to be lived in reasonable comfort and security. From this it follows that we should hesitate before we take up an alarmist note. The evidence is well presented in the March edition of *Marriage Guidance,* but I think it is possible to see that evidence not as confirming some disturbing departure from established and trusted ways of being, but as witnessing to couples' wishes to struggle towards ways of being together which they can bear without too great stress, and that they are being impeded in those struggles by social and institutional norms of behaviour. It is instructive to note point 8 in the editorial of *Marriage Guidance* to which I have already referred. Citing Dyer and Berlin's *Living Together*, the editor says that 'marriage *eventually* became an acceptable option to most (cohabiting couples) either because they wanted to have children or because of the reluctance of legal and social institutions to recognise a relationship other than one established by a marriage contract.' Our legal and social norms do, in fact, stigmatise almost every way that people find possible to share their lives with each other except lifelong marriage. While this is not the sole reason for the alarm many people feel when they discover that a rising number of their fellows are unable to live in that way, it would nevertheless be helpful if those legal and social norms could be changed.

There is some sign that the law, or at any rate the courts, are moving in that direction in some recent judgements concerning cohabiting partnerships. If we were able to recognise that relationships exist legitimately on a number of very different bases and that people are struggling to find the way which suits them, then we might find it possible to fashion our social and legal institutions in such a way that those in difficulty in that search are helped rather than impeded.

Finally, and perhaps most difficult of all, it suggests that we should recognise that a greater element of choice exists in the way that relationships are formed and maintained than we have been wont to allow. Choice in these matters has usually meant only shall it be this partner or that? Now it may mean not just with which partner but is it to be on a permanent basis? or an arrangement which may terminate after a longer or shorter spell? with one or more partners? Or in relation to parenthood it may mean a choice of not having a partner at all in any recognised sense, even though a child or children may be born. Such choices have always existed and have been made but usually with a sense of stigmatisation for those who have made them. They have hardly ever been seen as attempts to come to terms with the many conflicts involved or as a consequence of strivings to grow and develop. The recognition of choices as a way in which people try to reconcile the contradictions in their lives and feelings suggests also that it may be idealistic to expect choices to be made once and for all in terms of relationships. It may be a happy accident if they are, but it is possible to see in the course of people's lives that a process of working at the problems of living is going on.

This may mean that past choices may become invalid or that they may have been made from an excess of anxiety which impedes the attainment of gratification for either partner. Inter-racial marriages, for example, are frequently like this and are often not sustainable because they involve a choice which inhibits the achievement of important life objectives. It is facile to see this as failure, but I think it is better to see it as an attempt to reconcile painful conflicts which will continue to be struggled with in order to find a satisfactory resolution. It seems to me that we would do better as a community to help those attempting to make these difficult choices, recognising the joy and the pain involved while people work out their destiny.

References

1 Home Office: *Marriage Matters.* A Consultative Document by the Working Party on Marriage Guidance, HMSO, 1979

2 Sutherland, J D (ed): *Towards Community Mental Health,* Tavistock Publications, 1971

3 Erikson, E: *Childhood and Society,* Penguin Books, 1965

4 Bowlby, J: *Attachment & Loss, Vol. II, Attachment,* Hogarth Press, 1977

5 Meredith: *Song in Modern Love,* Constable, 1922

6 Weiss, R: *Couple Relationships in the Couple,* Marie Corbin (ed), Penguin Books, 1978

7 Auden, W H: 'Lay Your Sleeping Head', in *Poems from New Writing 1936-1946,* John Lehman, 1946

Discussion

What the discussion during the day certainly brought out is the fact that it is not only an individual's or couple's expectations of marriage which have to be considered—it is also society's expectations. One cannot look at how individuals of the opposite sex relate in marriage without seeing that in the context of how the sexes relate more generally in our society. Society's expectations provide a normative framework which is restrictive yet stable and secure. To challenge the restrictions is also to challenge the security.

Various other themes emerged. The importance of education in personal relationships; the relative importance of emotional or ideological factors, as opposed to practical constraints, in marriage and marriage preparation; the high personal expectations with which people approach marriage; the continual change of individual and joint needs within a marriage.

Education in personal relationships was seen to be related to the articulation of feelings and ideas. The paired opposites that Robert Morley talked about were partly conscious and partly unconscious, but more often the latter. Penny Mansfield did not think any of the 68 couples seen had actually compared notes of what they expected from marriage beforehand, although the question of job priority had sometimes been raised. In general, the women in that survey were more inclined to want to talk about problems and feelings. The fact of being interviewed privately and at length for the purpose of the research gave the men in particular a chance to talk which they might never otherwise have had. If expectations are largely unconscious and unspoken, then maybe what is needed is to help people to articulate their ideas and thus bring them into focus.

Education should be seen as a continual process, extending over the whole of the life cycle and covering practical aspects of marriage, such as finance, as well as emotional and sexual aspects. The researchers were surprised to find that newly-wed couples discussed practicalities and independence from their parents' home far more than the emotional fulfilment of being married or their partners' qualities.

Only 13 of the 68 couples had lived together before getting married, but almost all of them had slept together. After marriage, many found themselves isolated and cut off from their old friends and contacts. As Nicholas Tyndall said in his concluding remarks, facts like this must affect how education work and preparation for marriage is carried out. What is needed is honesty and openness.

Penny Mansfield talked about the high personal expectations which people now have of marriage, and not, as at the beginning of the century, of their socially defined selves in marriage. Robert Morley said that marriage, as defined in our society, is only one of a variety of relationships which may suit different people, but it is the one which is socially acceptable and not stigmatised, and thus a relationship in which high expectations are invested. If people expect a lot out of marriage, except to be 'happy', and find that this is not always the case, then there is assumed to be a problem with the marriage, and too often this is thought to be insurmountable.

This raised the issue of working at problems in relationships—the importance of accepting change, adaptability, communication, and give and take in marriage. Implicit in much of what was said, but not spelt out until almost the end of the discussion, was the fact that people, their needs and expectations, are constantly changing over time, and this, maybe, is the dilemma of marriage.

Manchester, 18 May 1982:

Children—For Better, For Worse?

Chairman   *The Lady Avebury, BSc,* Chairman, The National Marriage Guidance Council. Assistant Director, MIND.

Speakers   *Christopher Clulow, BA,* Deputy Chairman and Senior Caseworker, Institute of Marital Studies. Author of *To Have and to Hold,* Aberdeen University Press.

   Eric Cooper, Assistant Chief Probation Officer, Merseyside Probation Service, with responsibility for training. Formerly Senior Divorce Courts Welfare Officer, Merseyside.

Introduction

Patterns and expectations of marriage are currently undergoing rapid change, and children are the victims—and sometimes the cause—of conflict in the family.

Christopher Clulow of the Institute of Marital Studies was talking about the effect the birth of children may have on a couple and their relationship. Linked to this was discussion of the need for education and support for couples before, during and after the birth of children.

Eric Cooper, assistant chief probation officer for Merseyside, helped us look at the other side of the coin—the problems children may face rather than the problems they may bring. Not all children come from 'ideal type' families, and their various family backgrounds may present difficulties.

Christopher Clulow

Children—For Better, For Worse?

There is a story told of a misunderstanding between husband and wife about the purpose of married life. They thought they had fulfilled their marriage vows only after completing a very large family. When questioned about this they explained they had promised to have—and to hold—at least eight children: four better and four worse!

I want to talk about two relationships. The first is the relationship between children and parents—paying particular attention to the effect of children on their parents' marriage. The second is the relationship between care givers and care receivers in the wider family of society. Here I would like to say something about the dilemmas facing those who wish to translate into action the very good case that can be made for services to prepare people for parenthood. In both connections I shall be drawing upon work done by myself and colleagues at the Institute of Marital Studies relating to the very early stages of family life, the period following the birth of a first baby.

If you have been watching any of the many recent serialisations of classic fiction on television—for example, the recently completed *A Woman in White* —it will hardly have escaped your notice that relationships between men and women, and between parents and children, need to be understood against the social background of the day. The landscape of family life in the 1980s is therefore a suitable starting point for considering the relationship between children and marriage.

It is just ten months since I pressed into Hyde Park, on a warm summer's night, amongst thousands of others, under the roving eye of a television airship and the criss-cross patterns of searchlights, to watch the fireworks and strain to hear, unfortunately without success, the more or less accompanying music of Handel which heralded the Big Wedding of 1981. It can now be only a matter of weeks before the Prince and Princess of Wales announce the birth of their first child, and for the country, the primary significance of the event will be in terms of the future succession to the throne.

The royal wedding and birth, at least in their public aspects, are a hangover from sixteenth and seventeenth century patterns of marriage in this country.

At that period in our history marriage without children would have been unthinkable at least for the better-off, since an important part of its purpose was to maintain the family line through the eldest male descendant and so insure against the unwanted dispersal of property and influence. Because of what was at stake, the choice of marriage partner could not be left to the individual, and it was not uncommon for the views and preferences of the couple to be placed at the bottom of the list of considerations when a decision was being made. But then very much less was expected of marriage than is the case today, or was even by the late eighteenth century, when many of the values behind present-day family life were already well-established.

If children are no longer an essential part of marriage, there are indications that they remain a desirable part of the deal. Ninety per cent of first marriages produce children, but the number of children per family has declined. In the 1970s, although family size increased for the professional and intermediate classes, it fell in other social groups.[1] A preview of the 1980 American census results indicates that 'only children' are a very much more common phenomenon than ever before.[2] It will be interesting to see what is happening in our own country when the 1981 census results become available. Despite the trend towards smaller families, it seems that we still live in a pro-natalist society. Some couples do choose to remain childless—or child-free as they will say—but the very existence of an organisation like BON (the British Organisation for Non-Parenthood), whose main purpose is to eliminate the cultural bias against couples who choose not to have children, is itself evidence of the prevailing view that marriage and children are part of the same package.

Within that package there have been changes. Over recent years the age at which women have their first child has gradually increased. Part of this delay in starting a family can be understood in terms of a shift in sexual roles which, for women, has opened up employment alternatives and additions to being a wife or mother. In the past 20 years the number of women in paid employment has risen by two and a half million, whereas the corresponding figure for men has dropped by half a million.

As it has become more common for women to work, so the number of *mothers* in paid employment has increased. Between 1961 and 1977, the proportion of mothers of pre-school-aged children who went out to work increased from 12 per cent to 27 per cent.[3] There is some evidence that half of all mothers in Britain have had at least one job before their children reach school age (Hughes *et al,* 1980), and that a substantial number of mothers who do not go out to work would like to do so.[4] Maternal employment has been one of several factors which has resulted in a growing demand for pre-school day care facilities, in effect a plea that the care of very young children should not be the exclusive responsibility of the family—and for family one can often read 'the mother'.

While children are commonly viewed as an integral part of the marital package, it is now more questionable whether the parents' marriage is essential to the decision to have and to bring up children. Despite the availability of abortion and the decline in the number of children placed for adoption, illegitimacy has continued to increase in the 1970s. Twelve per cent of live births registered in England and Wales in 1980 occurred outside marriage as compared with 8 per cent in the early 1970s.[5] Slightly over half of these births

30

were registered by both parents which suggests an increase in the number of stable cohabiting partnerships during that period. There has also been a formidable increase in the number of single-parent families in the past 15 years. It is estimated today that one in ten families in this country have only one resident parent.

This last point draws attention to what has been the most publicised trend in the family over recent years: the increase in the divorce rate. England and Wales have the highest divorce rate in the EEC. In 1980 there were 12 divorces for every thousand marriages as compared with two per thousand in 1961. In 1979 six out of ten divorcing couples had children under 16 years old; one quarter of these were under five. That is not to say that the children involved will all remain in one-parent families; today, 34 per cent of all marriages are remarriages. You may be interested to know that this figure is almost precisely the same as that recorded for Manchester in the 1650s. The difference lies in the fact that divorce has now replaced death as the principal reason for ending these first marriages.[6]

There is no certain way of knowing whether the divorce figures mean there has been an increase in marital unhappiness or disaffection with marriage as an institution, or whether we are now seeing what was previously obscured by a legislative veil. What seems likely is that there has been a shift away from child-centred values towards companionability, personal development and satisfaction of the couple as the core values underlying contemporary expectations of marriage.[7]

As a public and as a private institution marriage has a particularly onerous burden to bear in times of rapid social and technological change. In an economic world which often demands a mobile labour force, and which can sometimes leave husbands and school-leavers out of a job while wives remain employed, the socialising function of families becomes even more difficult. Not only must parents transmit values from one generation to the next, they must adapt those values to a changing world. Three hundred years ago the influence of the community, religion and the law provided a degree of certainty about rules of behaviour in relationships which is not present today. Emancipation from the rules of the past has resulted in greater emphasis being placed upon the rights of individuals, and upon personal responsibility for the way choice is exercised.

Marriage as a private institution is a relatively recent phenomenon. Even within the present century it was common for family members to share their home with servants, lodgers and apprentices. Commenting upon the private pressures on modern marriage, an English anthropologist compared our system with that of a small society in these terms:

> In a small scale society a man may be able to love his mother, respect his sister, hate his father's sister and copulate with his wife. In our system, he does all four with his wife.[8]

She used the phrase 'pressure cooker marriage' to draw attention to a situation where contemporary marriage is called upon to do more than ever before at a time when it has arguably never been supported less.

It is against a background of changing attitudes towards marriage, divorce and the organisation of family life that the relationship between children and marriage must be viewed. In a period of general social change, the specific uncertainties and stresses associated with change for the individual assume particular significance. It is to the stresses which have been linked with the transition to parenthood that I would now like to turn.

The folk wisdom of our time propounds that children create families, that they help to maintain marriages and ensure their stability (with the corollary that divorce is more likely amongst the childless), and that children are a source of emotional satisfaction. They offer a second chance, make effort and sacrifice worthwhile, and give a sense of immortality.[9] Is there any validation for these beliefs?

I want to go straight to the horse's mouth and present some anecdotal accounts of early family life. These comments were collected by questionnaire from couples, most of whom were reviewing their first year of life as parents. Here's what some have said in connection with some common flashpoints in marriage.

Rows

We never used to argue until the baby was born, but she took so much out of us the first six to eight months, due to illness and not needing sleep, that we just felt we needed to take out the pent up feelings on someone.

I have found we don't argue like we used to. I think I used to argue to liven things up. Now things are too lively all the time. We haven't had a big row since he was born.

Sex

We did not have sex for about ten weeks, and it was a while after that before I enjoyed it. The main reasons for not having intercourse were continual tiredness and soreness. My husband would stay up and give the baby his late night feed, and I went to bed early and got up to give the early morning feed, so we weren't often awake in bed at the same time.

Our problem was my inability to explain what I felt or meant and my husband's persistent requests for explanations because of his inability to understand the mental and physical changes taking place during and after pregnancy. For my husband, because I had had a baby I should then have been quite normal apart from 'post natal depression' which he was all ready to deal with. When I wasn't co-operative about sexual intercourse he thought that I didn't care.

Money

Although money is freely handed between us, it's not the same as having a regular income that you've earned.

I work both from choice and necessity. Although I do not feel guilty about having made this decision I find that other people, particularly mothers, tend to assume that if I can cope with a baby, full-time job, house, etc. . . . . I must either do things badly or be exceptional. I resent this.

Child care

My husband has more patience than me with the baby. But he had more contact with children. Children never interested me before my own child was born.

We all get up at 8.30 am and while my wife changes the baby I get dressed, then come down for breakfast (coffee and toast), then rush out. I get home by about five, by which time dinner's been made for the baby and I. The baby goes to bed at seven.

We feel that the baby has in fact benefitted from an excellent child-minder . . . I needed to go back to work early (i.e. two months) before I became too settled in home/baby routine.

The verdicts:

I find the baby has brought us closer together. When we were both working we were like two individuals. Now we have something to share apart from our home.

I can honestly say that for the first six months the baby put a tremendous strain on both my husband and myself as individuals and on our marriage as well.

For me I have new-found security and a strength I didn't realise I had. I feel much more direct as a person. There is a strong bond in our relationship which was not there before. We are now a family and that's a new and positive feeling.

In these comments there is expression of both the labour pains, if I may call them such, which preface the birth of a new family, and yet the view that children do, indeed, create families.

What may be less expected and less accessible to conscious expression, is the way children re-create families. At the Institute of Marital Studies we have become very impressed by how powerfully the past can speak in the present, so that even a happy event like birth may take parents by surprise when they find themselves in the grip of feelings and behaviour which they cannot reconcile with their conscious wishes. In my view, one of the changes new parents have to manage is a greater degree of separateness in their relationship than before. The experience of normal separateness in a close adult relationship is capable of unsettling people who, as children, may have experienced painful separations—perhaps through illness, displacement by other children or the divorce of parents. It is not difficult to understand how a real child can stir the 'child' within the parent to life. Quite unconsciously the baby may then be regarded as a rival, a persecutor or harsh critic; equally the partner may take on similar properties and be regarded as parent or child to the spouse, with whatever implications that might have.

The recovery of childhood through one's own children is, of course, one of the great rewards of parenthood when it operates benignly—and by saying this I do not wish to suggest that less settling manifestations of the past are to be regretted if they can be contained, for how else are we to learn and re-learn through experience and so develop? As illustration of the power of parenthood to re-create—as well as create—families, I thought I would include a brief piece of prose written by Laurie Lee.

Laurie Lee wrote *The First Born* in celebration of his own daughter, capturing some of the early hopes and ideals which children bring:

For the rest, may she be my own salvation, for any man's child is his second chance. In this role I see her leading me back to my beginnings, re-opening rooms I'd locked and forgotten, stirring the dust in my mind by re-asking the big questions—as any child can do.

Children do indeed create, and re-create families, but since every family has its own story to tell, the nature of that experience can be very different for different people. There is no guarantee, for instance, that children will create marital bliss. So what of the second piece of folk wisdom which I referred to, proposing that children make for more stable marriages? If stability is defined as not ending up in the divorce court quite so soon, there may be some evidence to support this. For example, in 1979 the median duration of marriage for divorcing couples with children under 16 was just over 11 years as compared with eight years for those without children.[10] However, I understand from those more practised in interpreting statistics than I am that the picture is not as clear as it might at first appear. The one association which does hold good is that marriages following closely upon the conception of a child (where parents are often very young) and marriages which produce children very early on are statistically more prone to breakdown than others.

An interpretation of this link is that marriages are less likely to flounder when couples have established a partnership together before having children, and when getting married and starting a family does not become confused with other milestones in life—like leaving home. What cannot be done is to argue that marriage will necessarily be more stable if couples delay having children. The potential meaning of a conception is unlimited. The baby may be a manifestation of love, it may mark the end of a disagreement, it may be to save a marriage and provide a common interest, or to tie a partner down. The child can equally be the symbol of unity or disunity in marriage, the product of a reasoned decision, or a pawn in the conscious and unconscious power politics of a relationship.

The last strand of folk wisdom proposes that children bring satisfaction and fulfilment to marriage. Here, again, it is difficult to respond with a clear yes or no. To match the changes in the relationship between the sexes and expectations of marriage which have featured in the last 25 years there have been a growing number of studies (mainly American) which suggest that marital satisfaction decreases with children. These studies suggest that satisfaction drops during the pre-school years of children, picks up when they are at school, dips again during adolescence and subsequently climbs. On a graph the pattern would resemble a shallow letter 'W'. However, it is not altogether clear whether it is necessarily the children who are primarily responsible for these variations, or other factors, like the 'corrosion of time', to use one researcher's phrase.[11]

Other studies have suggested that marital satisfaction increases with children. To explain this apparent contradiction it has been suggested[12] that insofar as children separate parents, the more a couple have shared interests and lives, the more prone they will be to experience the presence of children as an intrusion in their relationship. Conversely, the more differentiated the partnership, the more likely that children will provide a common focus and point of interest, resulting in greater satisfaction deriving from the partnership than before.

Perhaps the one general conclusion that can be drawn is that marriage must change in some ways if all the members of the newly-formed family unit are to thrive. Stress, which is part of the experience of parenthood, can, up to a point, be understood as both simulus for, and manifestation of, a process of change.

But to stop there would be to deny that stress can destroy as well as create. It would also be to deny that there are ways of easing the transition to parenthood, and that there is a role for those of us who, from our different agencies, have a professional as well as personal responsibility to care. It is to some of the dilemmas facing the care-givers that I now want to turn attention.

For the purpose of illustration let us use the phenomenon of post-natal depression, perhaps one of the best known 'conditions' attached to parenthood, which it would be good to alleviate. Post-natal depression is a blanket term which covers a spectrum ranging from the 'blues' at its most common, to post-puerperal psychosis at its most uncommon; it is estimated that between 70 per cent and 80 per cent of women experience the upset in the first week or so of the baby's life known as the 'blues', as compared with three in every thousand mothers who have a psychotic episode requiring a temporary stay in hospital. Within the blanket term of post-natal depression falls the chronic depression which was found to affect one in three mothers in a London study of working-class families with pre-school aged children.[13] Before intervention can be planned in relation to any of these states, some view must be formed as to what causes the depression, and its meaning for those involved. Here, the same phenomenon may be capable of upholding different interpretations, and the interpretation adopted as the basis for action is likely to indicate the professional orientation of the care-giver as much as anything else: we see what we are trained to see.

In order to compare like with like, consider the contrasting explanations which have been given for the 'blues'. Medical explanations will often be in terms of the bio-chemical changes occurring in a woman's body following birth which can affect mood, and in particular the drop in progesterone levels once the placenta has been discharged.[14, 15] With this view the correct action is either to let nature takes its course, or to consider hormonal therapy to restore the body's chemical balance. Another view, this time sociological, sees the blues in terms of an iatrogenic illness, a side effect of 'the colonisation of birth by medicine',[16] to use the words of Ann Oakley. In this study, published three years ago, a statistically significant association was found to exist between the 'blues' and high technology births. The implications for intervention here are quite different: the system of care becomes the patient. Some conflict is then inevitable between, for example, the views of Dr Odent and his team, as presented on a recent television programme, that birth can be made both safe and satisfying by assisting mothers to do things the way they want with the minimum of technological aid, and the prevailing view in this country which sees medical technology as essential to the health and safety of both mother and child.

When there are conflicting interpretations of the same problem there is a tendency for professionals to polarise allegiance and prepare the ground either for battle, or for a studious deafness in relation to the voices coming from opposing camps. Such responses may result in a view of human life which is mechanistic, reducing emotions, in the example I gave, either to the status of a side product of bio-chemical interaction or to an end result of helplessness induced by a misguided social world. I find it exciting that in the world of the physical sciences researchers are beginning to define their role as participants rather than observers, emphasising the multi-causal nature of events, and a systemic view of reality, which studies inter-relationships rather than component parts.[17] With this view, the role of parents or patients in securing treatment which may or may not be good for them, cannot be discounted. Speaking about a philosophy for the caring professions, Sutherland[18] argues that the aim of providing good professional care is the same as providing good parenting— not, as some would have it, to infantalise people, but to enable them to secure independence.

He goes on to speak about the seductive but regressive effects of a collusion between, on the one hand, services which feel they must provide solutions, and on the other, a community which expects such solutions to be readily available. The pressing problem is always that of enabling an informed exchange to take place between the interested parties—whether they are on the giving or receiving end of services—and he argues that this might well be a target of an educational drive on both the public and the professions.

There is, similarly, room for bringing together different views in the way *persisting* depression has been understood. For example, psychiatric views have often stressed the intra-psychic effects of motherhood on women, paying particular attention to the nature of the internalised relationship between a mother and her own mother. Paradoxically, the worse that relationship is believed to be, the greater is the tendency to foster idealised standards of motherhood against which the new mother stands self-condemned, or others stand condemned by her in her place. Idealisation is a product of a psychological process in which good and bad qualities are separated out from each other and often attributed to different people, in much the same way as children distinguish between fairies and witches.

On the other hand, sociologists have argued that the all-sacrificing good mother is less the product of the mind than a cultural stereotype of femininity, rendering women defenceless against the pressures and demands of the outside world without renouncing their claim to their own sex. Here the remedy lies not in providing psychotherapy for a woman to come to terms with herself but, in Hannah Gavron's words[19] in making '. . . some deliberate attempt to reintegrate women in all their many roles with the central activities of society'.

Some links between social and psychological factors were made in the study of the social origins of depression which I referred to earlier. Here, an event like birth was not of itself considered sufficient explanation of depression amongst young mothers, but only in conjunction with pre-disposing factors like poor housing, an unsupportive marriage, unemployment or financial difficulties. Similar circumstances affect people in different ways, according to how well or ill-protected they are against the impact of events. I would add that events have a particular significance for individuals according to their life experience. Here an interaction between the inner world of the psyche and the outer world manifested in social relationships becomes a proper object of attention.

Causal complexity of this kind does not make the task of those who seek to prepare people for parenthood easy. Given the particular professional perspective of the Institute of Marital Studies, which no doubt makes us susceptible to the weight of evidence indicating that the quality of marriage is an important factor determining what sort of experiences men and women are likely to have in making the transition to parenthood, we decided that couples, rather than either parent, should be the object of any preparative endeavours in which we were to be involved. It was not just that the resources of marriage were likely to be taxed by events; the relationship worked both ways. We argued that by mobilising the resources of a couple, by encouraging communication between partners and with the relevant services, there was potential for reducing the wear and tear of what can be a stressful period. To this end we offered evening discussion groups for couples in four London family health centres. The groups were run in collaboration with health visitors as an extension of existing pre-natal programmes of education, although they also operated in the early months of parenthood. In addition we ran workshops for the health visitors themselves, in which recurring issues arising out of their individual contact with families were identified and examined. Finally we sent a questionnaire to all the couples whose first pregnancy was notified to the health centres where we were working in a 15 month period, enquiring about the effect of a baby on their lives and relationships, and particularly their marriage.

It is beyond the scope of this paper to examine the findings of the project, which are in any case to be published shortly,[20] but perhaps I can talk you through some of the questions connected with preparation for parenthood which were raised for us as a result of our experience.

In a climate of social diversity and change, what is it that couples need to know when embarking upon family life? This question is more easily answered in relation to a primarily physical process like giving birth, than it is in relation to what is involved when a family increases in size from two to three-plus members. Some types of information are more unchanging and subject to generalisation than others. The developments which take place in a woman's body during pregnancy can be described in a relatively straightforward way, as can the process of labour and delivery. Medical and dietary advice can be combined with information about where to go and what to expect from particular services. Up to a point it is possible to teach parentcraft skills. Direct information and advice of this kind, can be, and are, invaluable to prospective parents.

Yet the process of conveying even this information is not necessarily straightforward. Information is always given within a social context (even if by way of radio or television). A degree of power is vested in the giver and there is an assumption of need in the recipient. How information is given and received within that relationship will affect how the participants react to their prescribed roles. An assumption on the part of the specialist that he or she must always be 'in the know' may blind him or her to the resources of those who are there to listen. Anxiety, or feelings about authority, may prompt the listener either unquestioningly to accept, or to reject the advice proferred. Information is never a neutral commodity. It will be credited or discredited according to its source, the manner in which it is given, and its particular meaning to the individual. It is a fallacy to approach preparation for parenthood as if people are purely rational, duty-bound adults needing only to be better informed to succeed in their roles.

This point becomes even more telling when information concerns personal feelings and family relationships. One person will regard the experience of another with caution, and will not unquestioningly accept its relevance to him or herself. And quite right too. The idiosyncratic nature of experience, and the complexity of factors which go to make up what an event means for a person, are likely to subject general statements about, for example, the likely effects of children on marriage, to the criticism of being either simplistic or irrelevant. A creative outcome is likely to depend upon some spark, some matching preoccupation, which can bring an exchange of views to life so that similar and different experiences can be shared with safety.

In these circumstances, and with regard to the personal effects of change, it is difficult to know whether it is information which is important, or the relationship within which that information is conveyed. What is certain is that the way a relationship is established, to whom it is offered, and the didactic or responsive nature of the interaction which follows will, in itself, constitute an important message. Preparation classes organised in the daytime and directed towards mothers are a clear statement about the relevance of women, but relative unimportance of men, to this stage of parenthood. In terms of what these classes offer at present the message may be entirely appropriate. It was in connection with the absence of couple-oriented services linked to the wider needs of family members that we wanted to question such implicit communications, given how important marriage can be for parental adaptation.

Once the nature of the relationship between services and parents is accepted as being an integral part of any communication, the issue can no longer be confined to what couples need to know (needs which, to some extent, they can be relied upon to articulate for themselves), but must include what practitioners need to know. In our work we made three broad assumptions which I believe hold good for psychosocial transitions generally: first, there will be ambivalence about change however much it is consciously desired; second, the extent of the gap between expectation and experience will be significant in determining the ease with which change is accomplished; and third, there will be some interaction between a person's inner resources and the resources actually available in the community which will affect how far and in what ways available help is taken up and used.

These assumptions are easier to state than to act upon. It is not feasible, even were it desirable, to chart the course which couples might take in becoming parents since the passage can be made in so many different ways. Nor is the problem simply one of catering for a diversity of circumstances. The expectations we have about the future, our tendency to look on either the bright or gloomy side of life, our degree of resistance to change and preference to go it alone, for example, stem from emotional conviction born of life experience. They reflect learned ways of coping with uncertainty which may or may not facilitate adaptation, but which go some way to define us as people. Programmes designed to promote emotional health in the family are likely to be approached with caution because they might challenge cherished assumptions which we hold about ourselves and our world.

The question of how to establish a link between parents and services then becomes every bit as important as what happens once that relationship is established. Here we run into more problems. Surveys of existing ante-natal classes suggest that it is the older, better-educated middle-class women who attend. By and large this is a fair description of the social characteristics of those who attended the discussion groups we ran. A situation exists where those identified as most vulnerable to transitional stress (young mothers and those from social classes IV and V) are least likely to make use of available services. Some have suggested that this is because the services are hard to reach, others that parents are hard to reach. It has been claimed that social factors provide sufficient explanation, that working class families find preventive services irrelevant to their needs and alien, and that they are more likely to turn to relatives and friends for support—that they have not the 'future orientation' of the middle class, and so the desire to plan ahead which allows for preparative services to assume some relevance.

If that is so, it is also true that when one feels fragile or vulnerable, the prospect of intervention from outside can be threatening. Those strong enough to talk openly about their uncertainties and anxiety about change are likely to cope better than those who assume they will have no problems. They are also those who will see help as being relevant. Paradoxically, those least willing to talk, and perhaps most anxious, may avoid using whatever help is available. I have already mentioned that a poor experience of being parented can lead to the setting of unrealistically high standards by those least-equipped to match them. Failure to live up to an ideal may result in self-imposed isolation, in order to conceal failure from oneself and from others. A social climate which promotes only a rosy view of parenthood and values self-sufficiency (something which is rather different from autonomy) may serve to compound the problem.

Of course, when considering why some invitations are taken up and others are not, the characteristics of the host are as important as those of the guest. At present there is a break in the continuity of care afforded by services to new parents. Since nearly all first-time mothers have their babies in hospital most will attend there for medical examinations and preparation classes. Once the baby is born, and a mother discharged home, a different set of people take over. The break in continuity coincides almost precisely with the event of birth.

When we were deciding where to hold our discussion groups we opted for community health centres in preference to hospitals, despite the considerable numerical advantage we would have had if we had drawn upon couples attending hospital clinics. The reason for swimming against the tide in this way lay in our feeling that hospitals do not generally provide the sort of environment which is conducive to what we wanted to do. Anecdotal accounts of busy clinics, long waits for brief examinations, and contradictory advice received from ever-changing staff, were sufficiently frequent to question whether, either from the parents' or our point of view, hospitals constituted a facilitating environment for what was intended. Hospitals are large, complex, and, to many people, intimidating institutions, which trade in illness and disability rather than health and life.

Because we wished to offer some continuity between pregnancy and the early months of parenthood there were additional practical difficulties resulting from the fact that once a baby is born, and his mother returned home, there is unlikely to be further contact with the hospital apart from a routine check-up six weeks after birth. We considered that even if it were appropriate and desirable for hospitals to be active in the post-natal period, there would be considerable practical difficulties in maintaining the link for parents who lived a long way away.

One of our findings was that of the four centres we worked in, it was the two smaller ones, with access to fewer parents, which were most successful in attracting and holding couples to the discussion groups. Their smaller size meant it was easier to integrate the groups with other activities in the centre. A closer working partnership was established between ourselves and the health visitors with whom we worked since they were directly involved in and therefore identified with the project. Because of the smaller number involved they could more often make direct personal contact with couples when issuing invitations. Our experience was that small and personal meant a better take-up rate of the service we were offering.

It will be apparent that I have moved towards considering the unspoken messages which services convey as well as their conscious intent. From my own experience of being a parent, and from my involvement with the 'first baby project', I would say that different experiences of parenthood have to be lived to be discovered and cannot effectively be learned about in advance. The pressing need is to provide conditions in which people can acknowledge their experience, good and bad. The question for preparation schemes is only partly what parents need to know about how it might be for them (information which they might well choose to overlook or discard if it unsettles prevailing assumptions on the basis that 'this won't happen to me'), and more to do with how experience is managed.

Here the network of relationships inside and outside the family is crucial if experience is to be usefully integrated, and not concealed or denied for fear of its unacceptability. Those of us working from a medical, social or psychiatric base, professionally or in a voluntary capacity, form part of the family's social environment. To some extent we are the extended family of the 1980s. If there can be continuity in the services we offer in times of personal change or crisis, if we can avoid assuming that staff are interchangeable when it comes to offering a personal service, and if we can listen without having to act precipitately, we may develop the sort of relationships in which there is trust, and which stand the best chance of being used by families in assimilating change.

References

1 Central Statistical Office: *Social Trends,* HMSO, 1982

2 Watson, P: Report in *The Times,* 1.3.82

3 Central Statistical Office: *Social Trends,* HMSO, 1979

4 Bone, M: *Pre-School Children and Their Need for Day Care,* HMSO, 1977

5 Central Statistical Office (1982): op cit

6 Stone, L: *The Family, Sex and Marriage in England 1500-1800,* Weidenfeld and Nicolson, 1977

7 Home Office/DHSS: *Marriage Matters,* HMSO, 1979

8 Bott, E: 'Family and Crisis' in Sutherland, JD (ed): *Towards Community Mental Health,* Tavistock, 1978

9 Mattinson, J: *Childlessness,* unpublished papers, Institute of Marital Studies, 1981

10 Central Statistical Office (1982): op cit

11 Blood, RO and Wolfe, DM: *The Dynamics of Married Living,* Glencoe, Indiana: Free Press, 1960

12 Feldman, H: 'The Effects of Children on the Family' in Michael, A (ed): *Family Issues of Employed Women in Europe and America,* Leider, Brill, 1971

13 Brown, GW and Harris, T: *Social Origins of Depression,* Tavistock, 1978

14 Hamilton, JA: *Postpartum Psychiatric Problems,* St. Louis: Mosby, 1962

15 Dalton, K: 'Prospective Study into Puerperal Depression', *Br Journ Psych,* 118, 689-692, 1971

16 Oakley A: *Becoming a Mother,* Martin Robertson, 1979

17 Capra, F: 'Einstein and the Buddha', *The Listener,* 11 and 18.3.82

18 Sutherland, JD: *The Psychodynamic Image of Man',* Malcolm Millar Lecture, Aberdeen University Press, 1980

19 Gavron, H: *The Captive Wife,* Pelican, 1968

20 Clulow, CF: *To Have and to Hold: Marriage, the first baby and preparing couples for parenthood,* Aberdeen University Press, 1982

Eric Cooper

Children and Marriage

W e are all extremely familiar with the ways in which marriage is changing at the present time and I am sure we would agree on some of the contributing factors: changing economic conditions; redundancy; unemployment; increased life expectancy; the availability of contraception and other medical and legal services. These all play their part in the present process. I want to dwell for a moment on the cultural climate in which those things have made their impact.

I read once in a book on counselling that when the couple come to you in the counselling room they are, in fact, dramatising the conflicts and tensions of a whole culture in transition, and I think there is probably something in that. If we look back at the 1960s, we recall that those times were characterised by a tremendous thrust for freedom—freedom for women; freedom for students; freedom for 'blacks' and freedom for 'gays'. Freedom for all kinds of social and cultural groups. The message of that decade seemed to be that freedom for its own sake was infinitely to be desired. Towards the end, however, and into the 70s, there was an increasing amount of doubt and pessimism. Revelations about the abuse of power by individuals and governments, Watergate, Vietnam, industrial strife—all combined to lead us into the days of recession and stagnation when all those apparently unlimited horizons that were so eagerly sought in the 60s were suddenly closed down. Freedom for its own sake seemed less desirable and we began to ask about the purpose of freedom.

Some historians take the view that marriage suffered from a kind of cultural lag, in that the traditional form which was geared to an agricultural economy took an enormous length of time to adapt itself to the industrial society. Whilst the required changes and adaptations were being absorbed, the situation was already changing further as we moved into what some people have called the 'post-industrial society'. In this view, marriage has been overtaken by a cultural change which was quite unexpected in its nature and scope, whilst still making adjustments to an earlier situation. It is not surprising, therefore, that important questions are being asked about the marital relationship and, as a consequence, about the purpose and direction of counselling.

It is not only marriage that has changed, but counselling also, reflecting the different and changing views of the relationship itself. Originally, as I understand it, counselling was based on the belief that difficulties in the marital relationship were attributable to something within the individual whereby counselling became a very private process between an individual spouse and a counsellor in which the individual's history, expectations and perceptions were examined and linked. As the theory of marital and family relationship developed, counselling moved rather more into the position where it would focus on what was happening between people. The interaction between spouses became the focal point and counselling techniques reflected this new belief. In some places counselling has moved on even from there and groups of couples may now be seen. In the absence of old certainties about the marital relationship, and counselling as well, we seem to be left with little more, at the present time, than 'cereal packet marriage'—the ad man's perfect vision of the ideal family!

We were reminded by Christopher Clulow that, statistically speaking, the earlier one marries (and particularly if there is a child already on the way), the more one runs the risk of a breakdown in the marital relationship. We were also reminded of the symbolism that children may carry for their parents which counsellors really need to understand and use. Children do have enormous significance for their parents—the origins and associations, the layers of meaning, are usually very deeply buried but are sometimes reflected in the names that they bear, and the myths in which they are caught up. Parents themselves may often see children differently from each other. The importance of a child for one parent may be completely hidden from the other.

Marriage has always been more rewarding for men than for women. There is now, however, an extremely powerful thrust for change in the marital relationship, particularly arising out of the change in female aspirations. As women pursue greater individual fulfilment they may become much less bound by the constricting roles of mother and traditional wife. This seems to be an extremely hopeful and optimistic trend, but once again we have to remind ourselves that we are being overtaken by very wide-ranging and significant events. It is ironic that at the precise moment when women's aspirations are broadening out and moving on, for a significant proportion of the married male population the opportunities and horizons are closing down. It is now not unusual to find oneself dealing with a relationship in which the woman demands fulfilment and purpose and the man is faced with the horror of redundancy and long-term unemployment.

The position of children is also changing, I believe. They seem to be much less dependent on their parents for many things. There are available to children today sources of information, stimulation and play which simply did not exist and were quite unaccepted only 15 years ago. One of the effects of that, I think, is that children are becoming less dependent on their parents at a much earlier developmental stage, and a loss of idealism (particularly in relation to parents) may now be observed in quite young children.

It is a fact, however, that one quarter of all married couples nowadays actually have no children at all. Couples who decide not to have children may see them as a hindrance to their own enlarged expectations, or, conversely, an economic drain in times of increasing hardship. That so many married people see parenthood as less necessary, and less desirable, indicates that there has been a significant cultural change whereby it is now possible for those people to say quite clearly that they do not wish to take on a role which society would have thrust upon them much more forcibly and unavoidably only a short time ago. We must expect the proportion of childless couples to increase.

I want to move on now to the wider question of marital stress and breakdown. There are three things at least which are quite indisputable about modern marriage and I would like us to examine them in turn. Firstly we know that more marriages than ever are breaking down and resulting in separation or divorce; secondly, we know that more people are now cohabiting before marriage—particularly before remarriage; and thirdly, we know that there are more people than ever marrying for the second or third time. It sounds from these facts as though the more marriage proves itself to be unsatisfactory, the more we desire it, which appears to be a very odd situation indeed! Before we look at these three factors, I want to pose some questions about why they have come to exist.

First of all, I wonder whether the statistics referred to arise from a growing conviction that marriage itself is intrinsically desirable and good but that individuals have simply been unlucky. Perhaps people now believe that it is in order to try relationships until you acquire a satisfactory one. Berger and Kellner say that marriage has become so important to the individual that only the perfect union will now suffice. It is an interesting thought that the very worrying divorce statistics may (according to this view) arise out of greater demands being made on the marital relationship rather than the reverse.

The second possibility that occurs to me is that perhaps these factors indicate a wholesale rejection of the romantic ideal—the notion that there is somebody special for you and all you have to do is find him or her. We were referring earlier to the way in which the nation responded to the marriage of Prince Charles and what it was that it touched in all of us. Perhaps if we as a people believe less and less in the romantic ideal we need our fairy stories more and more. In this view, one of the contributing factors might be thought to be a more realistic view of the impact that children make upon a marital relationship.

Thirdly, it occurs to me that perhaps we are becoming increasingly reluctant to grapple with the pain of change and adjustments that committed relationships require. It is, of course, much easier to escape a painful situation now than it was just a few years ago. The implications of this tendency, if it is true, are particularly serious for children. How else are children going to learn that you can face difficulty and pain, go through it, and survive, unless they see their parents do that? We run the risk of perpetuating the problem through our children.

The last thought I have on these factors is that perhaps it marks the death of real commitment. Have we embarked on a process of putting personal commitment to anyone or anything much lower in the balance, and raised into greater prominence our personal needs, demands and ambitions? That might not be quite so obscure as it sounds. I was reading recently in an American publication that there are now some schools of counselling which are saying that it is no longer valid to think in terms of marital problems—marriage *is* the problem and those counsellors who take that view naturally take a significantly different approach to their counselling. Their bias is to help the individual to survive as a whole person in spite of being married. One study reported: 'marriage, with its unpredictable future and its lack of shared history, is the most unstable of all social relationships.'

Now let me come to the first of those three facts which are statistically proven and examine them in a little more detail. The first of the three things that we know is that marriages are breaking down at an increasingly rapid rate. Divorce is the new death. We were reminded that this can be statistically proven. The difference of course is that, unlike death, we have no formal social rituals relating to divorce and we are consequently placed in a situation where we literally do not know how to behave. Some of the conciliation services which are now available will undoubtedly have identified the need for a good deal of detailed work on this matter. The rate of increase in divorce has reached the point where extremely sober people are beginning to express alarm and worry. In one of the legal journals recently, an official was expressing the view that divorce has become too easy to obtain. Certainly I have personally heard of cases in which petitioners have taken a rather insubstantial petition to one court rather than another in order to have it approved by one registrar in the belief that it would not have got past another.

The dilemma for people contemplating divorce, in the light of the considerable social and cultural changes to which we have referred, is 'shall I sacrifice myself for the marriage's sake?', which was largely the position up to only ten years ago, or 'shall I sacrifice the marriage for my sake?' The impact of all this on children is difficult to estimate, but at long last we now have access to a major study by Wallerstein and Kelly called *Surviving the Break-up*,[1] which is a study of American middle-class divorced families, and particularly their children, over a period of many years. Clearly those findings should be translated to the British scene (and particularly the British working class scene) with caution. But, nevertheless, I want to draw your attention to four findings which they offer in relation to children and divorce.

Firstly, Wallerstein and Kelly say that less than ten per cent of the children in their sample found any relief whatsoever in their parents' decision to divorce, despite the high incidence of physical violence which was taking place in the marriage. This suggests that there may be a conflict of interests between what parents want to do about a difficult relationship and what the children need. You may not find that surprising, but in the context of our enormous increase in divorce, we may be observing the increasing dominance of parental wishes over children's needs.

Secondly, they say that they found little evidence that the parents' wish to escape from a difficult marriage was shared by the children. They discovered that when parents are very unhappy, children can be relatively happy, and I must say, from observations that we have made in our own conciliation interview room, that I would agree with that. The dominant impression of my own conciliation work during the last two years has been the incredible resilience of children in situations of high drama and conflict.

Thirdly, Wallerstein and Kelly say that when divorce does take place, what children regret losing more than anything else is the clear structure of two parents, an identifiable home and siblings (if there are any). It is the lack of structure which children seem to suffer most.

Fourthly, children's ability to cope, they suggest, is strengthened by understanding that the divorce is a serious remedy for an important problem. If they can grasp that, their coping is enhanced, but if it is unplanned or unexplained, it is a very severe burden which they have to carry—with long-term consequences. This may be something which we have known for a very long time, both from our own experience and from any good novel. We had in our interview room fairly recently, two people who were in the process of divorcing. They were both still living under the same roof and they had two girls aged about 13 and eight. They were perfectly delightful children. The parents were perfectly delightful people. They came to us because they had to decide who was going to leave the matrimonial home and therefore, as a consequence, who was going to look after the children—who was going to have custody of the children. And before we had been there very long it became clear that these people were in the process of conducting an extremely civilised divorce. They were speaking to each other sympathetically, apologetically; they were clearly taking great trouble to avoid making any damaging references to anything that had happened in the past. They were bending over backwards to explain that anything that had to be said was not to be understood as an attack on the other. And what they failed to see was that all the time this was going on, these two lovely girls were in the room, quietly sobbing, so that it took us a while also to latch onto the fact that this was happening. It seems that the unspoken rules constructed around their breakdown and divorce made it impossible for the girls to make any reference to the hurt, the pain, the difficulty, the anxiety about the future, which they were bottling up inside themselves, and containing with some difficulty. I drew this to the attention of the parents, and what happened was very interesting. Because those two people did not in fact divorce: they became reconciled.

It seems to me that there is something very important about this question of informing the children appropriately about what you want to do and why you want to do it. I think we would all agree that children's ability to cope can only be improved by that kind of openness. An even worse situation than the one I have described can occur when what is happening to the family is misrepresented. Shortly after the incident I have mentioned, we were in the same room with two parents and two boys, and it became immediately clear that there was something very odd between them. The children were cowed and apprehensive—but of us rather than the parents. We established that the father had told the boys that this was a court and they really had to be extremely careful because important decisions were going to be made; but he did not tell them what the decisions were or why they were necessary.

The second thing we know as a fact is that cohabitation prior to marriage is increasing significantly, particularly before second marriage. Sociological theory shows that in the eyes of society two married people become a pair. We are encouraged by society's inducements and constraints to have an image of ourselves which primarily relates to the place that we have within the pairing. Because of this, when breakdown and separation occurs, the individual finds himself in a social vacuum. One's condition is not easily recognised or explained. To be involved in a marital breakdown is to be left in a 'no man's land' at the mercy of powerful institutionalised influences—legal, social, economic and political—which have the effect of making you form another pairing, because to be a pair is to have identity, purpose and recognition. This process was described in Nicky Hart's book *When Marriage Ends*[2] as 'status passage'.

Another piece of research indicates that three out of every five women who eventually marry again enter into a cohabitation first. When questioned about this, it seems that they married because of the perceived social pressures to do so rather than to continue cohabiting, in order to ease the pressures—particularly in relation to children. We therefore need to consider whether the remarriage statistics mask and misrepresent the attitudes of individuals towards remarriage. It is not necessarily safe to assume that marriage is as popular as the statistics would seem to indicate. If those social pressures (which were felt so keenly by single, separated individuals or cohabiting pairs) did not exist, there are some indications that the remarriage statistics would be quite different. There is a further factor here which relates to what I believe to be a widely held assumption—that, in order to obtain a favourable decision about the custody of children after marital breakdown, to be seen to be once more involved in an apparently stable and paired relationship, is vastly superior than to have single parent status. The conservatism of the courts sometimes seems to dictate that children ought to be with the mother on purely biological grounds, although many different but enlightened decisions are now being made, particularly in the high courts. Nevertheless, it is a heavy additional burden to feel these pressures at the very time when one is having to cope with massive personal adjustments, probably involving severe depression and deap-seated anger. This can hardly be the most fruitful time for establishing new relationships.

Thirdly, let us look briefly at the question of remarriage itself. The traditional view of marriage as life-long monogomy is now giving way to an acceptance of what one might call 'serial monogomy'; in other words, that one moves from one married relationship to another, and increasingly to a third. Clearly there are problems here for children. Take the simple example of parents who divorce. Where each parent remarries and has children by the new partner, see if you can establish clearly in your mind, or write down on paper, the complexities of roles and relationships in which each of those individuals becomes involved. The skills required to counsel blended families are really quite considerable. Some work has now started and is beginning to be written up, but much more is needed. For children, of course, one could take the view that 'serial monogomy' could be a source of great richness; that they have so many more relations to care for them, so many more models to observe, that the need later to make choices and judgements will be helped by the availability of a whole range of experiences which would have been unavailable to them in the normal run of events. What we see in divorce court welfare, however, is the more negative side of this. The individuals who, for many reasons, are not able to find the capacity to cope with the complexity and who are left in a minefield of emotional confusion.

It is interesting, I think, that all this coincides with the development in psychological theory about the importance of a child's attachments. We seem to be moving away from the old model whereby a child was thought to be particularly enriched by a lifetime's connection with his biological parents, towards a slightly different view, which is that what matters is the hierarchy of attachment figures, biological or otherwise, by which a child is surrounded. When that subtle development is applied to questions of fostering, adoption, wardship, the removal and rehabilitation of children, one gets into a very complex area of developing legal and social work practice.

Let me conclude by saying this. It seems to me that simultaneously with all the changes that I have mentioned in the last decade or more, there are two associated and quite disturbing developments in relation to children which we must acknowledge. First of all, the numbers of children being committed to care, being sentenced to detention centres and borstals are increasing alarmingly. The second development is that at the same time as that is happening, social casework with children and families has declined due to the squeezing of resources, especially in local authorities, where, paradoxically, they have the statutory duty to anticipate and prevent the very problems that are placing children in those institutions. It seems to me that, with the benefit of hindsight in a year or two's time, we might have to conclude that at the present moment we are presiding over the death of casework. For political, economic and social reasons we are being put in a position now where the only time the distress of children will be acknowledged is at divorce, or at the point at which no preventive work can be done.

I wonder whether we are getting to the point where the state, because of the increasing complexity of the parental task and the dimunition of resources to provide assistance to parents, is taking over far too readily as parent to any child who is seen to have a problem. I personally know of many, many families where committal to care, or the sending to borstal or to detention centre of a child, is regarded almost as a necessary developmental phase, by means of which the parents are relieved from the tension and pain of having to see them through the adolescent transition. If children are increasingly going through their formative years in institutions run by the state, what will be the future of marriage and family life in another two decades?

I want to close with a word of caution about conciliation. If there is any truth at all in any of these last few things I have been saying about resources and about the state as parents, then it seems to me that the current tendency to view conciliation facilities, however they may be organised, as some kind of panacea for all family, marital and childish ills, is gravely mistaken. What we might be involved in, in fact, is the setting up of a last-ditch service into which the necessary funds and resources will be poured, but they will be taken from the point at which they would have achieved much, much more, and that is in the realm of detection and prevention at a much earlier stage. Money and resources which are now being taken away from the social services may well come back to mop up the mess when families have broken down and children are on their way to institutions.

References

1 Wallerstein, J and Kelly, J: *Surviving the Break-up: How children and parents cope with divorce,* Grant McIntyre, 1980
2 Hart, N: *When Marriage Ends,* Tavistock, 1976

Discussion

As Nicholas Tyndall said in his concluding remarks, one major difficulty in discussing subjects like marriage and family life lies in distinguishing fact from belief. Deeply held convictions about stable marriage and family life are valid as long as they are acknowledged as convictions. But, whatever different ideals of marriage people had, there was an overall recognition of the fact that marriage had indeed changed. Contemporary patterns of marriage present a series of complex choices and models which children may find confusing.

The example of children in reconstituted or blended families was used. Apart from the problems children may have relating to step-parents, there is the often overlooked difficulty of two sets of children relating to each other. It may be at adolescence that these step-children's problems become apparent, but it is hard to judge how much of this difficulty with step-children or foster children is due to their being in a 'different' kind of family situation from the 'ideal type' nuclear family, and how much is due merely to adolescent rebellion.

There are no answers to questions about what marriage should be like, or what sort of upbringing, whether in a family or not, is best for children. One participant said he had spent six good years in an orphanage and this helped to restore the balance of the discussion.

It is not what happens to couples, families, and children that really matters. Of paramount importance is how transitions are made. It was suggested that since divorce involves a major transition for both partners, it should be marked by *rites de passage*. The ritualisation of divorce might help people to come to terms with their decision and consequent new status, and thereby save children from becoming involved in their parents' guilt. Looking not at how divorce must affect children, but how the transition can be made easier for all concerned.

One way of easing transitions may be through education, for parenthood as well as for marriage. But there are problems of 'when' and 'how'. Christopher Clulow suggested that trying to teach parenting to adolescents is made more difficult by the fact that at that age they are trying to dissociate themselves from their own parents.

As a head teacher pointed out, teachers themselves are not trained to help parents cope with their children. Self-help groups may be one of the best ways of reaching and educating people in such skills. Not being based on an authoritarian model, they are more likely to appeal to all kinds of people.

There was great emphasis on the services which are provided to help people, whether in education, in preventive work, or in dealing with difficulties. These services should either give continuity of care, which was what, with special references to natal care, Christoper Clulow was asking for; or, as Eric Cooper suggested, they should be able to collaborate much better as a professional network.

The final thought from Nicholas Tyndall was about 'pressure-cooker marriage'. If marriage in modern society is indeed 'pressure-cooker marriage', (E Bott, 1971), then we must remember that despite the potential for disaster, pressure cookers actually cook food very well if you get it right.

Change in Marriage—Reality and Implications

Chairman   *Clare Jones,* Lecturer in Applied Social Studies (Psychology), University of Bristol.

Speakers   *Jacqueline Burgoyne,* Senior Lecturer, Department of Applied Social Studies, Sheffield City Polytechnic. Special research interests, second marriages and reconstituted families.

Dr Ruth Coles, MB, ChB, Brook Advisory Centre, Bristol Richmond Hill Clinic, Bristol.

Lisa Parkinson, MA, CQSW, Co-ordinator, Bristol Courts Family Conciliation Service.

Dr W Ll Parry-Jones, MA, MD, MRC, Consultant in Charge, Highfield Family and Adolescent Unit. Clinical Lecturer, Psychiatry, University of Oxford.

Introduction

The chairman, Clare Jones, said in her introduction that we were going through a period of social transition of a very dramatic kind. There is confusion in our society today as to the definition of 'family', and this confusion can be seen in changing, and increasingly varied, patterns of behaviour. There is no longer such an obvious progression for young people to follow; from courtship to engagement to marriage to parenthood. As rules, rituals and progressions are eroded, people are faced with a wider personal choice of behaviour and of belief which may mean greater cumulative stress.

Jacqueline Burgoyne, the main speaker, took up the theme and talked about change and changing expectations of marriage and partnership. The speakers who followed, Dr Ruth Coles, Lisa Parkinson and Dr W Ll Parry-Jones, were considering how professional services should adapt to these changes.

Jacqueline Burgoyne

Contemporary Expectations of Marriage and Partnership

Introduction

In this paper I want to consider a variety of material which bears upon marriage and contemporary family life with the intention of setting up a framework within which we might begin to judge the significance of the kinds of changes which have prompted NMGC to organise this series of study days. Such a framework may also help us, whether as members of occupations directly concerned with the family, or more personally, to consider the policy and practice implications of such changes. As a social scientist with interests in research on various aspects of marriage and partnership I believe that the 'promise' of social science lies in its capacity to stimulate us to ask better, more searching questions, to locate the issue or problem in a broader social, economic and political context so that we begin to see the links between apparently unrelated phenomena. Thirdly, the social sciences provide us with a useful set of rules, which stress the necessity for neutral observation and judgement based, where possible, on impartially collected evidence.

Sources of data on marriage and partnership

Any attempt to judge the significance of marriage and partnership requires a variety of different sorts of information and perspectives. We need answers to the when? how much? how many? questions in order to establish patterns and potential trends. For this we depend on publicly-collected 'official' statistics of the kind very ably summarised in Lesley Rimmer's recent booklet for the Study Commission on the Family.[1] Such data often confirms changes and trends which we may have already observed ourselves but they can also dispel many myths. For example, if we were to rely on the images of the family transmitted in the media we would greatly overestimate the number of people living in family groups consisting of two adults and their dependent children (the proportion of all households of this type has, in fact, dropped from 38% to 31% between 1961 and 1975.[2]) When I first became interested in marriage and divorce some six or seven years ago, the students whom I taught tended to underestimate considerably the number of people involved in divorce. More recently this has changed because of periodic moral parries in the press and on radio and television about divorce trends of the 'Divorce-Crazy Britain' variety. Many people now tend to overestimate the likelihood of couples marrying now being divorced in ten years time.

However, such data tell us nothing about changing beliefs and values, or what people believe marriage and family life *should* be like. It is frequently asserted by social commentators, politicians and moral entrepreneurs of many different persuasions that values have changed but there is little empirical evidence of these changes. Last year, as part of our continuing interest in people's expectations of marriage, David Clark and I organised a survey of public beliefs about various aspects of marriage, divorce and cohabitation, financed by the Medical Research Council. This survey was carried out in Sheffield and Aberdeen to provide background data for other qualitative studies we are both working on. I shall refer to some of the preliminary findings later in this paper and also to a recent *Sunday Times* survey. However, the obstacles and challenges we confronted when we began to design the interview schedule and, later, to consider the significance of the results, raised important general questions about such 'public moralities of the family' as Voysey has called them.[3] As she worked on an investigation of the experiences of a group of parents with handicapped children she came to the conclusion that the parents' answers to many of her questions told her very little about the actual experience of caring for a handicapped child but a great deal about what it *ought* to be like. Their conceptions of a 'normal' or 'happy' family were derived, in part at least, from the advice-givers, doctors, health visitors, social workers and teachers they had been in contact with because of their child's disability, and they saw the research interviews they took part in as another public context in which they had to render an account of themselves as parents.

This analysis draws our attention to the critical relationship between personal experience, the public contexts which shape the lives of individuals, and the kinds of socially-constructed knowledge to which we refer to make sense of our experiences. The social scientist cannot judge the extent to which any given individual's personal values and moral codes—his or her conscience—are affected by such public moralities, but we can try to trace how such public moralities have changed and offer some tentative observations about how differential access and exposure to 'expert' advice and ideologies of various kinds may have helped to create a diversity of expectations about marriage and its alternatives.

We also have access to other kinds of information about the personal experiences of individuals from a variety of other sources. Journalists writing books about marriage (this seems to be something of a growth industry) present case studies of 'ordinary' people as well as those who, because of their work, have a stock of accumulated secondhand experiences of other people's marriages: marriage guidance counsellors, doctors, psychiatrists and, on occasion, social researchers such as myself. In addition, each of us has an understanding of family life based on our own experiences and our observation of other people's. The chief problem with such material is the caution we must exercise about drawing general conclusions from inevitably limited evidence. However qualitative material of this kind should not be rejected as it provides us with an insight as to how people make sense of their personal lives in a way that large-scale 'representative' surveys never can.

Finally, I want to introduce material which illustrates how social science can help us to ask better questions through consideration of how changes in beliefs and values about marriage and partnership are related to other broad social, economic and ideological changes. Such analysis will not of itself provide answers to the problems of policy and practice posed by present trends, but I believe it will help us to locate connections between changes in beliefs and values, which are neither obvious nor immediately apparent.

The scope of this paper and a note on terminology

The NMGC study days all focus on change in marriage, but it is difficult to separate a consideration of marriage from that of parenthood. They are inextricably interlinked in our personal experience, and in more general public beliefs about family life. It is commonly suggested that children 'make a marriage' and for many involuntarily infertile couples an important aspect of their personal anguish is frustration that they are unable to 'complete' or 'round off' their commitment as partners through having and caring for children together. However, as I shall be suggesting later, in a variety of ways high divorce rates have made explicit the fact that adults' expectations of, and investment in, partnership may change whilst their commitments as parents persist over a considerable time span.

Terms like 'marriage and partnership' illustrate the same recognition of the increasing diversity of partnerships and household arrangements which has prompted NMGC, concerned primarily with marriage and family relationships, to extend its services to all those 'who have difficulties or anxieties in their marriages or other personal relationships.'[4] In this paper I want to use the terms 'couple' and 'coupledom' to refer to the common features of partnerships whether legal or cohabiting. In the introduction to a book entitled *Couples,* Marie Corbin, a social anthropologist, describes how:

> Many people involved in sexual relations come to think of themselves as a unit, a couple . . . Because they define themselves as 'a couple' they may feel that they 'ought' to behave in certain ways. The Unit may also be recognised, even insisted upon, by other people. Invitations may be issued to the couple: couples may be bracketed in people's minds as 'nice' or 'odd' and so on; one person may be treated as representative of the other or they may be regarded as interchangeable.
>
> This conceptual bonding is made easier if the couple may be neatly or simply labelled. In our society this seldom happens unless they are married . . . But the fact remains that two people may be a couple without being married and an individual may be married without being part of a couple.[5]

Demographic changes: the social consequences of people being more likely to marry than in the past and to live longer after they have done so

Although there have been fluctuations in marriage rates and some changes in the most popular ages for first marriage, all but a very small proportion of the population will have been married at some stage in their life, with most first marriages taking place between partners in the early twenties.[6] Husbands are most commonly two years older than their wives as well as being slightly better educated, earning slightly more, and even slightly taller! Such material demonstrates how statistical norms—the most frequently occurring case—are transferred into social norms about what constitutes the 'normal', 'natural' or 'best' pattern of relationships.

In the mid-nineteenth century a considerably lower proportion of the population were married at any given time. Professional men were advised to delay marriage at least until the age of 30 and society made provision for this group of influential single men through clubs in London and the provincial cities and a variety of commercial leisure facilities, including, of course, access to prostitutes.[7] Women of all social classes were less likely to marry than women are today because of unequal sex ratios. Their preoccupation with finding a partner in order to avoid the unenviable position of permanent spinsterhood is illustrated in many nineteenth century novels. Such anxieties persist today despite changes in the sex ratios; many young women still worry about being 'left on the shelf'. Today most people are in couple relationships so there is very little institutional or community provision for single people, except for clubs and other organisations whose manifest or implicit intention is to encourage people to find partners.

A woman friend of mine, a social worker in her late thirties, and a thoughtful and committed churchgoer, once described to me with great bitterness how her local church divided its social activities into groupings based on family status. As a single person she was consigned to a group called 'the odds and sods' which met in the vicarage on Sunday evenings! Thus the pressures on individuals to form couples are very strong and are undoubtedly accentuated by the sheer normality of coupledom. After a certain age you are unusual if you are still single, so that in subtle and complex ways, doubts may be raised about your eligibility, qualifications and performance in a couple relationship. This is an interactive process; single people are well aware of such negative stereotypes and frequently find themselves presenting some justification or explanation and may, somehow in the process, internalise a sense of failure and incompleteness which is mirrored in the material circumstances of many single people. Two may not be be able to 'live as cheaply as one' but the value of the economic exchange and support enjoyed within a shared domestic economy is, literally, incalculable.[8]

Further, whilst getting married and, to a lesser extent, living with someone, symbolises the end of adolescence and the achievement of adult status for those marrying for the first time, remarriage enables divorcees to regain some of the respectability and financial security they lost through marriage breakdown. For example, it is not uncommon for separated people to be given a lower credit rating simply because of their minority, 'deviant' marital status. Thus, to achieve or regain coupledom is, in a variety of ways, to associate oneself with the normality of an 'ordinary family life'.

One of the explanations frequently offered for increased rates of marriage breakdown is that marriages must survive for much longer because of increased life expectancy. There are certain problems about this kind of explanation, not least because most divorced people are now in the 25-29 age group and thus much younger than the widowed partners of a century ago. It is also not clear why longer marriages should *per se* lead to greater unhappiness or break down more frequently. There are, however, other related factors associated with greater longevity. Put simply, the longer couples live together the more critical events and changes they are likely to experience.

The following table illustrates the range and frequency of critical life events which a couple might experience during 40 years of marriage. Only a small minority of couples—unlike characters in 'soap operas'—face all these events and changes but they are all common 'everyday' experiences which generate potential for strain and conflict, opportunities for individuals to reassess their identity and relationships, and the possibility of personal change and growth.

Sequence of 'typical' critical life-events

Husband		Wife
	Earlier 'serious' relationships	
	'Living together'	
Married, age 24		Married, age 22
	Moving house	
		Leaves work because of
	Arrival of children	
Job change/ promotion		
	Illness/death of parents/in-laws	
		Returns to work
		Job change or
Involuntary		promotion
unemployment	Illness/death of close friend, sibling/sibling-in-law	
Own serious		Retirement
illness/death		Widowhood

Such a diagram might encourage us to consider what Bernard[9] has called the 'two marriages' contained in every couple relationship. Summarising a variety of research on marriage she concludes:

> There is by now a very considerable body of well-authenticated research to show that there really are two marriages in every marital unit, and that they do not always coincide.

From this diagram, for example, we might want to examine the interpersonal implications of social and economic changes in patterns of employment. Because of the recession there has been a sharp increase in the number of households where the wife is the main breadwinner. We also need to consider the sources of friendship and personal support available in each partner separately at different stages in the life cycle, and the times when they are most and least able to meet each others needs. We tend to see marriages in terms of snapshots—an image frozen in time—when a ciné film would be a more appropriate metaphor.

Changing beliefs and values: marriage and partnership as a public issue

As well as being one of our most significant sources of personal, intimate relationships and experiences, 'family life' is also a public matter, the subject of political debate and social comment of various kinds. Such debate is important not only because it may influence the political decisions, the policies and practices of institutions and organisations which shape aspects of family life, but also because the content of such debates, transmitted through the media, often becomes part of the thinking of individuals as they try to explain and make sense of their own experience of partnership and married life.

Let me illustrate this from the study of remarried couples David Clark and I have carried out in Sheffield.[10] As a society we designate our family life as part of the 'private sphere' of personal relationships. A symbolic area of everyday life in which we are really able to 'be ourselves', to express our individuality and to exercise the autonomy and freedom of choice which are frequently denied to us in the public sphere of work and formal relationships. Consequently the explanations offered for such 'personal troubles' tend to be individualistic in character, based on our own or other people's mistakes and inadequacies.[11]

However, some of the divorced people we interviewed for our remarriage study moved beyond such individualistic explanations as they tried to account for the break-up of their first marriage and the circumstances which led them to remarry.[12] As well as recognising the significance of personal factors, they frequently portrayed themselves as being part of a social trend or referred to changing public beliefs and values. On occasion such explanations appeared to neutralise some of the crushing sense of guilt and personal failure so frequently experienced by divorced people. They also tended to see the future more positively. Whilst the majority of the remarried couples in our study seemed determined to reconstitute 'normal family life' for themselves whatever the difficulties, others adopted a more 'progressive' stance. They emphasised the positive value of 'differentness', and the potential benefits to themselves and their childen of their unusual family domestic circumstances. For example, several divorced parents commented on the freedom they enjoyed when their children went on access visits to their non-custodial parent. For them, divorce was seen as a 'necessary evil', rather than a major disaster, and the public moralities of marriage and divorce to which they referred included a recognition of the increasing frequency, visibility and 'normality' of marriage breakdown.

There are, I would suggest, two significant and interrelated changes in beliefs about marriage which in their turn render high rates of marriage breakdown more explicable. The first is an increase in the emotional, interpersonal satisfactions which may be legitimately expected from coupledom and the second the increasing popularity of beliefs emphasising equality *between* partners within marriage. The results of a recent survey for *The Sunday Times* indicate the central importance of the interpersonal aspects of partnership. 'Being able to talk together about your feelings' was rated as the most important ingredient in a happy marriage by 62 per cent of the *Sunday Times* survey sample, whilst over 80 per cent of the people interviewed in our survey of family beliefs in Sheffield and Aberdeen cited emotional, interpersonal reasons in response to the question 'what, generally, do you think are the main reasons why people marry?'

The journalist who introduced the *Sunday Times* survey findings clearly had difficulty in interpreting the data on adultery. 'Right across the enquiry spectrum at least two people in three deplore the notion of married people sleeping with anyone other than their proper legal partner . . . although when it comes . . . to balancing the menu for a tolerable marriage, the little matter of sexual fidelity seems to rate very low indeed.'[13] We asked several questions in the Family Beliefs survey which shed some light on this, and also collected a good deal of relevant material in our remarriage study. Generally, it is not now the act of adultery itself which calls a marriage into question, but what it may signify for a particular partnership. Many of the divorced people in our remarriage study described how their marriage had deteriorated before they, or their partner, or both of them became involved with someone else; in an otherwise satisfactory relationship this would not necessarily have led to a final break. By the same token the divorcees in our study who portrayed themselves as initiating the breakdown of their marriage because of an affair with someone else, most often the person they were now married to, were at pains to describe an earlier deterioration in their partnership. As they 'grew apart', boredom and dissatisfaction gradually increased:

> . . . the marriage had been stale for probably four or five years, although I'd not realised what was wrong with it. I just thought it was me being funny, until I realised that there was a lot of things that weren't in the marriage that I really wanted. *(Mrs Dunwell)*

> I got to about thirty and you just think, is this all there is to life? . . . there's all the things you want to do and you've got someone who won't do them . . . I think you just gradually grow apart. *(Mrs Roberts)*

> When you've got established, when your house is organised, when your gardens are done, when everything's organised, then you start looking for something else and either turn to your wife or husband, whatever, or you turn to outside interests, sport or booze or whatever . . . *(Mr Pelham)*

Whilst some people began to search consciously for a potential new partner, others described new relationships which developed almost imperceptibly:

> It's true I liked Mary for years . . . It was only a process of time before we finished up where we did . . . It was mostly a process of friendly garden chatter . . . Later we was planning to meet even though we wouldn't admit it to each other . . . I've never taken a lot of notice of how it evolved: it just happened. *(Mr Roberts)*

Meeting someone who is experiencing similar dissatisfactions gives both parties an opportunity to re-evaluate their marriages. Mr Pelham, for example:

> Up until meeting Ann that was what sort of precipitated it, up until then it was what I thought was a normal marriage . . . it was just sort of drifting along . . . not unpleasantly. I mean it wasn't a ball all the time but it wasn't unpleasant . . . and then Ann came along and then, er, bang!

Thus, I want to suggest, albeit tentatively, from comments of this kind, that contemporary public moralities of marriage now provide a justification for leaving an unhappy unsatisfactory partnership in order to pursue a potentially more satisfying alternative. Present divorce arrangements intended as a 'decent burial' for dead marriages mirror such thinking but unfortunately offer little guidance to divorcing parents facing all the attendant difficulties of remaining parents whilst no longer partners. In the past decade popular versions of psychological theories stressing the importance of personal growth and change in adult life have received much greater attention,[14] especially in women's magazines and as part of the assumptions underlying advice offered by agony aunts, as well as in professional counselling. We found simplified versions of such beliefs in the explanations and personal justifications of several divorcees who were themselves unlikely to have had any *formal* access to thinking of this kind.

In the past decade 'the changing role of women' and appraisals of the degree of equality achieved by women in various spheres have become important public issues. Such debates are complex, not least because of the difficulty of obtaining reliable evidence about, for example, husbands' or wives' relative contribution to domestic labour and child care, but also because some women do not apparently want such equality anyway and thus evaluate their own circumstances, and those of women generally, rather differently. I would, however, want to argue that public moralities have changed so that many now pay lip service to beliefs which tend toward a greater commitment to equality whatever their private practices.

In the 1950s Young and Wilmott described how many of the working-class men of East London were reluctant to admit that they shared in child care and would not, for example, be seen pushing prams. Today in some neighbourhoods, occupational communities and strata of society verbal commitment to female equality has increased greatly, although sociological evidence about the domestic division of labour, patterns of child care and so on suggest that even amongst the middle classes, practices may have altered less than public ideology.[15] So some adults—both men and women—may now feel guilty and try to hide a traditional domestic division of labour or deep seated beliefs about gender roles at variance with the new orthodoxies of 'dual career families' and image of the 'superwoman' portrayed for example, in *Cosmopolitan* magazine.

Both of the changes in public beliefs I have described are likely to have profound effects upon individuals who, for a variety of reasons, begin to assess or reappraise their partnership which they have hitherto taken for granted. For example, couples who have been together for a decade or more drew up their 'contract of partnership' against a background of very different beliefs about gender differences and about marriage itself from those widely disseminated today. Similarly I am made very aware of the anxieties of many of my students, both men and women, in their late teens and early twenties, that their commitment to non-sexist policies and practices will be eroded if, as they describe it, they ever find themselves living on surburban housing estates.

Individualism and the growth of modern consciousness: coupledom as an escape from personal isolation

In this final section I want to consider some of the explanations offered by social scientists for our contemporary preoccupation with the 'self', personal relationships and, particularly, intimate partnerships. Commentators of differing political and philosophical perspectives describe how industrialisation brought in its train a symbolic division between the public sphere of work, the economy, politics and 'public life' and a private sphere of personal relationships.[16, 17]

The significance of this private sphere of family and personal relationships has been underlined by the growth of individualism, a range of moral, religious and social beliefs committed to the view that the value of a single member of society derives in part from the unique combination of characteristics, qualities and personal history which makes him/her qualitatively distinct from anyone else. Whilst many of our experiences and relationships in the public sphere diminish our sense of individuality, we characterise home, family, friendships and leisure as the context for our 'real' selves. Whilst we may act out roles in public, it is in our private lives, we claim, that we can really 'be ourselves'.

However, because of the changing, fragmented nature of social life in urban industrial societies, at any given time, our 'private life' may be located in a variety of disconnected groupings and relationships, or 'life worlds' as Berger and Kellner describe them. In addition social or geographical mobility, personal changes and critical life events may mean that we pass through different phases of life and networks of relationships which are linked only by the circumstances of our individual biographies. These quite separate life-worlds are linked over time in our personal biography and, as we pass from one to another in the course of our daily life, by our personal identity as individuals.

The dilemmas and potential pitfalls of this preoccupation with our individual identity and biography are well illustrated by the Walter Mitty film, and more recently in the work of Woody Allen. Acquiring a stable picture of ourselves as individuals and the composition of a well-rounded personal biography both require 'significant others' with whom we can test out our identity and who will listen as we make sense of the past, appraise the present and plan for the future. The innumerable conversations of courtship and coupledom are the contexts *par excellence* in which personal identities and biographies are confirmed and negotiated. In the context of physical intimacy—and hopefully acceptance—we tell our secrets and try to come to terms with disappointment and personal failures and if you stop to think about it, there are very few other well-signposted contexts in which we might expect to be allowed and encouraged to do so. Whilst therapeutic or even research interviews and 'chance' encounters with strangers provide temporary confiding relationships, we need to consider how access to friendships and contact with kin, thus providing a substitute or an addition to coupledom, varies for men and women at different stages in the life cycle.

We also need to raise questions about the ways in which idealised beliefs about coupledom as a totally consuming and entirely satisfying relationship may exacerbate feelings of loneliness and isolation. For example, many women of my generation have, in effect, 'rediscovered' friendships with women sometimes as a very indirect result of the women's movement. In our teens and early twenties we confronted life together, hunting in packs and

63

retiring to discuss tactics until first one then another found 'their' man and retreat into a relationship which, as we saw it then, quite properly demanded their first loyalty and greatest attention. Increasingly adult women, married, divorced and single are working, playing, sharing their lives together in a way which their male partners find disturbing and which, strange to say, I think they sometimes envy.

I would like to end by inviting your consideration of the ways in which we might, personally and professionally, promote the growth of a variety of the kinds of friendships which protect us from isolation and which would, ultimately, I believe, render our couple relationships more secure by diminishing the enormous and unrealistic range of expectations which are commonly attached to such partnerships.

References

1   Rimmer, L: *Families in Focus,* Study Commission on the Family, 1981
2   Ibid, p 61
3   Voysey, M: *A Constant Burden,* Routledge and Kegan Paul, 1975
4   National Marriage Guidance Council: *Aims, Beliefs and Organisation*
5   Corbin, M: *Couples,* Penguin, 1978, pp 13-14
6   Leete, R: *Changing Patterns of Family Formation and Dissolution,* OPCS, 1979
7   Banks, JA: *Prosperity and Parenthood,* Routledge and Kegan Paul, 1956
8   see Pahl, J: 'Patterns of Money Management in Marriage', *Journal of Social Policy,* vol. 9, part 3
9   Bernard, J: *The Future of Marriage,* Penguin, 1973
10 This investigation was financed initially by Sheffield City Polytechnic and completed with the aid of a grant from the Social Science Research Council. The support of both organisations is gratefully acknowledged
11 Mills, C Wright: *The Sociological Imagination,* Oxford, 1958
12 Burgoyne, J and Clark, D: 'Why Get Married Again?', *New Society,* 1980; and 'Starting Again: Problems and Expectations in Remarriage', *Marriage Guidance,* 1981
13 Wilsher, P: 'A Woman's Place?', *Sunday Times,* 2.5.82, pp 33-34
14 Lasch, C: *The Cult of Narcissism,* Abacus, 1980
15 Edgell, S: *Middle Class Couples,* Allen and Unwin, 1980
16 Zaretsky, E: *Capitalism, the Family and Personal Life,* Pluto Press, 1976
17 Berger, P and Kellner, H: *The Homeless Mind,* Penguin, 1974

Dr Ruth Coles

Education in Sexual and Personal Relationships

For more than 20 years I have worked in family planning and talked to people about their relationships and their sex lives and tried to help them with their problems. In dealing with the unresponsive woman, the impotent man, the non-consummated marriage and the unwanted pregnancies I have often felt that if only people had known the facts and understood the feelings and had healthier attitudes towards sexuality much unhappiness would have been avoided.

It is difficult to help the woman who is unresponsive to her partner because for 15, 20 or 25 years she has been taught that sex is dirty or sinful. This teaching was undoubtedly meant to help girls avoid the unacceptable disaster of illegitimate pregnancy at a time when sexuality and reproduction could not be separated. Perhaps it was the recognition of the strength of the sexual drive which instigated this very negative teaching, a feeling that the only way to prevent irresponsible reproduction was to forbid the sexuality which led to it. Once the negative tape was switched on marriage did not turn it off—sex cannot be sinful today and joyful tomorrow—and daughters who learnt their lesson well entered marriage as the frigid women their parents had made them.

It is difficult to help the impotent man for quite different reasons. He did not get pregnant so sex did not have to be forbidden. The lesson he learnt was that men were good at it all the time; he felt ashamed of his inadequacy and had to hide it; he could not possibly seek help. Fifteen or 20 years ago we used to hear about male sexual problems in our clinics through wives and we learnt to provide psychotherapy through these women because no man would ever darken our doors. Times have changed and today I see almost as many men as women in my psychosexual sessions.

Throughout history, man has attempted to separate sexuality from reproduction. Ancient man is said to have been unaware that intercourse was related to pregnancy. Intercourse was a common everyday occurrence and pregnancy and childbirth were much too important to be related to anything so ordinary. It was much more likely that impregnation was due to a spirit, a charm or even the wind. It was not long before the connection was recognised and attempts at fertility control are suggested by the presence of sheaths in the cave paintings. Contraception was a pretty hazardous business for many centuries because we were so ignorant. It was the 1930s before we began to understand physiology and it then seemed possible that we could find ways of preventing ovulation or interfering with the implantation of a fertilised ovum.

By 1960 we had virtually 100 per cent contraception in the form of the Pill. At last women could cease to be baby machines and sexuality could be considered more positively. We could begin to accept what Freud had told us many years before, that sexuality was present from birth, that it is a natural and instinctive part of our physiology which every individual has the right to enjoy. We had the opportunity to be more positive in teaching our children, the chance to teach them the pleasures of a real sharing relationship and the joy of sex. But who was going to teach them? Most adults, both parents and teachers, came from an era when table legs as well as human ones had had to remain covered. For centuries fertility had been worshipped, probably on the basis that as you could not avoid it you might as well join with enthusiasm. It was difficult to change rapidly, we were only beginning to consider our own sexuality and there were many inhibitions to overcome and thinking about the sexuality of our children was a bit frightening.

We began to learn about the sexuality of the young. Kinsey[1] had told us in the 1940s and 50s that the teens were the time of greatest sexuality but, if we believed it, we chose to ignore it. In 1965, Michael Schofield[2] carried out a survey of 2000 teenagers. In our anxiety about the young, many had said that there was not a virgin left by the sixth form. This proved to be untrue. At 16 years fewer than one in ten girls or boys were having intercourse, but by 17, 18 and 19 years many were sexually active. He found that only 27 per cent received any sex education from their mothers, fathers played no part at all.

In 1974 we learnt that teenagers had become more active sexually when Christine Farrell[3] told us that 51 per cent of teenagers were active, 22 per cent of them having intercourse before the age of 16 years. One in eight girls were having intercourse before the age of consent. She confirmed that it was still mum who did the educating, but for only 17 per cent of the boys and 32 per cent of the girls. She found that 90 per cent of parents thought they should tell their children about reproduction but only 50 per cent did. Seventy nine per cent thought they should tell their children about intercourse, but only 30 per cent did. Ninety two per cent of parents thought their children should be told about birth control—the ages at which it was suggested they should be told ranged from 10 to 17—49 per cent thought their children should be told the details of contraceptive methods, and 41 per cent thought that they should be the ones to give the information, though only 27 per cent had done so. The highest proportion of all, 97 per cent, thought their children should know about venereal diseases, 33 per cent thought that they should give the information and, surprise, 35 per cent had done so. It appears that we continue to be best at the negative and forbidding bits.

Christine Farell found that 96 per cent of parents agreed with sex education for their children in school, which makes you wonder why schools make such a fuss about getting parental permission for sex education when they do no such thing for other controversial subjects like English literature, history, religious instruction and even mathematics in its modern and traditional forms. If we

66

see education in its widest terms as preparation for life, then sex education must be very important. Many of our children will get by with very little knowledge of history or geography, but few will survive happily without considerable understanding of relationships and feelings. If you ask permission to provide sex education, you are likely to get opposition from parents who have difficulties with their own sexual feelings and are the least able to provide this teaching at home.

Although parents agree with sex education for their children, 72 per cent had no idea what they had been taught, so Christine Farrell told them. Fifty eight per cent of all teenagers had not been told about birth control. Of those who had received some sort of sex education at school:

> 78 per cent had been told about human reproduction
> 69 per cent had been told about animal reproduction
> 65 per cent had been told about sexual intercourse
> 57 per cent had been told about venereal disease
> 43 per cent had been told about personal relationships
> 40 per cent had been told about family and parenthood
> 23 per cent had been told about masturbation

It was good to see that humans had at last taken priority over rabbits and frogs. Unless you are sticking strictly to the mechanics, it is difficult to understand how you can talk about intercourse without talking about relationships—unless, of course, you have gone back to the rabbits and frogs! It does seem a pity that venereal disease was discussed more often than relationships; and that masturbation came bottom of the list when it must have been the form of sexual expression which many pupils were already experiencing and needed reassurance about.

We are now eight years on from Christine Farrell's survey and no doubt things continue to change and hopefully more children are receiving better sex education. We must not be complacent. From my daily contact with young people I am anxious about who teaches them and what they are taught. Last week I met a 17-year-old who wished to terminate her unplanned pregnancy. She had already seen a gynaecologist who was unable to do her termination because he had run out of beds. He told her this, and added: 'anyway, abortion is dicing with death'. In the same week this girl had attended a class at school where a nurse had given them a talk on contraception and told them that 'the pill is dicing with death'. This left my patient with little choice, but fortunately she did not believe either of them. We must be honest with our young people and not make the facts fit our feelings. Teachers of the young must come to terms with their own sexuality; they must pay no heed to how they were taught, if they were taught at all; they must shed their inhibitions about whether sexual activity is only suitable over a certain age because sometimes it is more suitable at 15 years than it is at 30; they must learn the facts and not distort them. Telling a girl about the side effects of the pill, which for most girls do not exist, with the idea that if you put her off the pill she will not have intercourse, does not work. You only increase the hazards, and she has intercourse without the protection of the pill.

As times change there are more and more teachers who have grown up without the inhibitions of the past and are more able to help the young. They must remember, as they try to talk about ideals to their pupils, that many of them may be living in situations where sex is not the joyful result of a good relationship, but where it is the source of rows, anger, unhappiness and unwanted pregnancies. We have to remain sensitive to the confusion this may produce for the child.

In talking about sex education in schools, I have no wish to decry the role of the parents, but simply to emphasise that the majority do not manage to carry out their good intentions. Parents find it difficult to allow their children to grow up. Their natural instincts make them wish to protect their offspring from the difficult, wicked adult world. Surprisingly they more readily expose them to the physical hazards of crossing the road, the rugby pitch, mountaineering, skiing and motorcycles. These exposures are supposed to increase their moral fibre and make men and women out of them, but parents recoil from any emotional exposure, from any finding out about love and relationships. Experimentation in this field is unacceptable, in any other it is essential. Mistakes, of course, may be disastrous but are more likely to be fatal when crossing the road or mountaineering. Of course we want to keep our children safe. I once heard a very sensible schoolmaster say that when his son wanted a motorbike he had had to save up for it himself but father had provided the crash helmet. It might be sensible for more parents to provide the crash helmet in the form of the pill.

Ideally, sex education starts in the cradle, long before there is any contact with teachers. Most mothers are aware that little boys have erections when they are being bathed or having their nappies changed and very soon the small boy obviously likes playing with his penis. A little girl's sexuality is not so immediately obvious, but sooner or later she will find her clitoris and enjoy it. The mother's reaction to this first evidence of sexuality is important: she may ignore it, allow it or forbid it. Many years ago when I was doing my obstetric training, and long before I had a family of my own, I was taught how to bath a newborn baby by a midwife. The baby was a boy, and when she came to put his nappy on, she told us always to make sure that the penis was downwards because it was not good for little boys to have them up; what a beginning and how forbidding!

Parents have the opportunity to provide sex education at just the right moment as the child matures, they have the chance to repeat the lessons at opportune moments. In school this is more difficult, and if information is given at a time when it is not relevant children will not listen or will not remember. To catch each child at the right moment, lessons must be repeated and you run the risk of harping on the subject until, to the parental question 'what did you do in school today?' the answer may be 'we did sex again with Miss So and So'.

At home, children learn from what they see as well as from what they are told. The sexual activities of the parents are private matters and no concern of the children, but ask any young adult what sort of sexual relationship their parents have and they will know because it is evident in the looks, the voice, the attitudes and the touching. There is nothing more constructive for the child than growing up with two parents living in a loving relationship, but we do not live in an ideal world and more than 20 per cent of our children do not have the privilege of growing up with two parents and many parental relationships are less than ideal. The child who grows up in a one parent family, whether this is due to death, divorce or illegitimacy, is disadvantaged from the start because there is no opportunity to work through the oedipal situation and go on to identify with the parent of one's own sex. Miserable marriages and changing relationships are no help either—only the best of parental relationships are good enough for our children—but parents are only human and a relationship which was good enough for marriage and procreation in the past needs a lot of luck, love, hard work and tolerance if it is going to produce good sexual adjustment in the next generation.

What is the result of sex education? Michael Schofield[4] went back and looked at the teenagers he had studied seven years before to see what effect their sex education had had. He concluded that the attitudes of these young people had changed but not what they did. They were more thoughtful about relationships, but did not always behave thoughtfully towards their partners; they thought pregnancies should be planned but did not always use contraception. All so illogical, but sex education is a long term business, attitudes change slowly and putting these attitudes into practice takes even longer. It is hard to stand by and watch the mistakes. There is more discussion of relationships today than there ever was in the past, and yet separation and divorce go on increasing. In the past, partners often stayed together for all the wrong reasons, but sometimes it gave them time to work through their difficulties and emerge with a stronger relationship. I worry that we are teaching our children too much about their rights and their individuality and not enough about their contribution to society and the sharing and the giving.

Our thoughts must always be with the young because they are our future, and bringing up the next generation is probably the most important thing that any adult does. It is a challenge and a commitment. Sex education has improved but it is not good enough. We must not be complacent and we must remember that it is a continually changing scene and what we teach today will be out of date tomorrow.

References

1 Kinsey, AC, Pomeroy, WB and Martin, CE: *Sexual Behaviour in the Human Male* and *Sexual Behaviour in the Human Female,* Philadelphia, Saunders, 1948 and 1953

2 Schofield, Michael: *The Sexual Behaviour of Young People,* Longmans, 1965

3 Farrell, Christine: *My Mother Said,* Routledge and Kegan Paul, 1978

4 Schofield, Michael: *The Sexual Behaviour of Young Adults,* Longmans, 1973

Dr W Ll Parry-Jones

The Eclectic Approach in Marital Counselling

From a historical standpoint, marriage is clearly an ever-changing phenomenon and, consequently, it is particularly important to retain an objective view of the process of bringing about change in disturbed marriage and the major tasks facing professionals who have responsibility for working with people in marital crisis. In this respect, the exercise of decontextualising distressed marriages and disentangling the enduring core of phenomena that are intrinsic in couple relationships allows certain common features to emerge. These include strategies for exchanging intimate personal gratification, the development and maintenance of a secure personal and sexual identity, establishing mutual acceptance, adapting to personal maturational changes and the setting up of mechanisms for coping with existential anxiety and loneliness.

It follows that it might be possible to formulate marital problems in terms of these fundamental interactive phenomena but, in practice, marital relationships are highly complex and, inevitably, remedial work with people experiencing marital problems is ambiguous and perplexing. Particular problems are generated by the fact that it is not easy to delineate clearly the scope of the field; there is no single, all-embracing conceptual framework; there is no widely agreed way of investigating, observing, describing and explaining marital problems and, finally, there is no all-purpose model for bringing about therapeutic change. It is to these facts and their implications for marriage guidance counsellors and others engaged in marital work that I want to address myself in this short paper.

I cannot start to be comprehensive in my coverage of the field, nor can I pretend to be neutral; like everyone else, I have beliefs about the best ways of going about things. For convenience, I am going to include counselling techniques under the broad heading of psychotherapy. It is not that I think these terms are interchangeable but they are sufficiently closely related for some general remarks to be made about them. Particularly if psychotherapy is used to refer to a variety of techniques for bringing about emotional, behavioural and cognitive changes, thereby relieving symptoms of distress and improving personal functioning.

If an historical view of psychotherapy is taken it becomes clear that ways of relieving personal suffering, allaying anxiety and changing behaviour have been used over the centuries based on the influence of the healer's personality, on wise counsel, or on various forms of reward and punishment, and these techniques have been explained according to the prevailing philosophies and beliefs and the ever-changing concepts of man's self-understanding. The history of marital and family therapy only extends over about 30 years but, during this time, marital counsellors and therapists, faced with the complexities of personal and interpersonal problems in marriage and all the changes that have taken place, have responded with intervention based on a plethora of theories, used to explain disharmony and to justify the remedies.

This is in line with what has been happening in the wider field of psychotherapy in that literally dozens of approaches can be encompassed under that heading, all with their fervent protagonists, appealing theories and plentiful partisan literature. Broadly, the individual treatments fall into three groups—psychoanalysis, behaviour therapy and humanistic-existential psychotherapy—the latter heading including a number of systems of which the best known is Rogerian client-centred psychotherapy which has had an important influence on counselling. Then there are the group therapies, including the encounter group movement and a multiplicity of family and marital approaches.

Faced with all these approaches it would be natural to turn next to outcome studies of effectiveness. This is particularly appropriate since the historical study of psychotherapy shows that one of its main characteristics over the centuries has been over-optimism about its benefits. Of course, outcome research is fraught with difficulties and this is not the time to take a detailed look at the studies themselves but I believe it is fair to say that, as yet, there is no convincing evidence of the superiority of any single form of psychotherapy in its immediate or long-term benefits.

However, there is a good deal of information about particular techniques which seem to be most effective in specific problems. We are beginning to know a great deal about some of the factors that seem to be related to good outcome in psychotherapy. For example, success appears to be related to the therapist's mobilisation of the client's expectations of help. It is probably true that expectations given need to be culturally meaningful and there is some evidence to suggest that whatever kinds of therapeutic activities are performed, effective intervention is the one that tends to reinforce the socio-culturally sanctioned coping mechanisms, even though these mechanisms vary greatly across different cultures. I think this finding is of great interest—it helps to explain the success of particular forms of treatment at particular times in particular cultures. Client-centred psychotherapy, for example, tends to reinforce notions of learning to solve one's own problems without therapist direction and this philosophy has had particular appeal in western society in recent decades. Similar explanations apply to the popularity of behaviourally-oriented sexual treatments in recent times.

The model of verbal self-explanation, derived orginally from psychoanalysis, still forms the basis of many psychotherapies and, of course, derivative links can be recognised between all forms of dynamic psychotherapy and the ideas of Sigmund Freud. But in the 1980s, we are well into an era that has seen the decline of the influence of psychoanalysis, with its classical focus on the intra-psychic events of individuals, and a rapid broadening of interest in behaviour and its determinants and in interpersonal relations, in groups, in marriage and the family. This shift of emphasis has generated a wide range of new theoretical models including, for example, those based on general systems theory and social learning theory. At the same time, there has been increasing emphasis on brief treatment and on focus, problem-oriented intervention. As I am sure you all know only too well, there has been a coincident explosion in the literature, making choice of reading a quite bewildering task.

We have no alternative but to respond to these changes, particularly in training. Preparation for marriage counselling and therapy has to reflect contemporary social, cultural and theoretical influences but, again, the historical perspective is a useful corrective when it shows that the indiscriminate use of any single approach can be a pitfall and impede progress. For this reason, I believe that eclecticism is essential and that prospective counsellors and therapists should be trained to be sceptical about strong alliances to particular schools and to be ever alert to the needs for change.

But, you may feel, surely the counsellor striving after eclecticism may be left in a very isolated position, paralysed into inactivity by having little or nothing to believe in? I do not think that this needs to be the case. On the contrary, I believe that an eclectic approach leaves the counsellor in a peculiarly strong position because of the ability to draw upon a wide range of explanatory models and forms of intervention. But a form of practice which encourages discretion in procedure, calls for a systematically planned approach including, broadly, alliance-building, data gathering, assessment and diagnosis and intervention. Alliance-building, in keeping with all other approaches, calls for all the traditional qualities of empathy, non-possessive warmth and non-judgemental acceptance of the client. Assessment needs to be based on a core of information that is not specific to one school of thought and should include particular emphasis on what is directly observable in marital interaction. Finally, intervention, whatever form it takes, needs to be based on the best working hypothesis about the nature of the problems and their likely outcome that can be assembled using all available information and drawing upon a wide variety of theoretical models.

As you can see, inherent in this approach is the acceptance of considerable responsibility for bringing about change in others. I think that this is inescapable but by this I do not mean that changes are prescribed for clients. Far from it, if you take the behavioural model, for example, the therapist can only proceed at the pace of the clients and within the range of changes that are seen as desirable and feasible by them. But the acceptance of responsibility does raise ethical issues and the necessity for it in counsellors has far-reaching implications for selection and training as well as for therapeutic practice. Within the Marriage Guidance Council, for example, it raises the question of how far part-time volunteer counsellors can be expected to accept significant levels of responsibility for effecting change in the lives of others and the extent to which the organisation can provide adequate training, personal supervision and professional support.

It is a reassuring fact that, within psychotherapy as a whole, there is good evidence that most therapists are eclectic in the consulting room whatever their partisan allegiances may be. Certainly, studies of theory and practice reveal many similarities between schools. In conclusion, at this time of transition attempts to collate and build upon the common features of divergent approaches, particularly dynamic and behavioural approaches are called for urgently. In this respect, I believe that there is a growing spirit of experimentation, collaboration and eclecticism, and if so—it holds an exciting prospect for the future.

Lisa Parkinson

Divorce and Families

Since 1978, the divorce rate in England and Wales has become the highest in the EEC. It has increased by 600 per cent in the last 20 years and the number of petitions filed annually has risen from 32,000 in 1961 to 172,000 in 1980.[1] Many divorcees remarry, and a third of all marriages in 1979 were remarriages for one or both partners. Burgoyne and Clark's research in Sheffield has shown that continuing conflicts over children and financial arrangements from a first marriage put great pressure on second marriages.[2] One in six divorces in 1980 were second divorces, for one or both partners.

The Study Commission on the Family has estimated that one in every five or six children is likely to experience his or her parents' divorce before reaching the age of 16.[3] Research findings have drawn attention to the adverse effects which are often associated with divorce, though not necessarily caused by it. Children suffer from the disrupted or diminished parenting which may occur if parents are absorbed in their own crisis. If conflict and insecurity are prolonged, children may show reactions in stress-related symptoms, depression, school failure or delinquency. It is crucial to understand the complex factors which may mitigate the impact of divorce on children and which can avoid or reduce the trauma of separation from one parent. A five-year study of 60 American families found that half the children were intensely afraid of being abandoned by their father, after he left home, and a third were afraid that their mother might disappear as well. The notion of a parentless household as a real possibility was not uncommon among children of various ages.[4]

The splitting up of a family is a high-risk situation for adults and children. It can bring necessary and constructive changes for one or more members of the family, or it can inflict deep psychological wounds, and the combination of emotional stress and practical problems can be overwhelming. The decision to end a marriage is not usually a mutual decision, planned and discussed by both partners. Very often, it is a unilateral decision taken by one partner against the other's wishes. Only a tiny fraction of divorces are ultimately fought out in the High Court (defended divorces cannot be heard in the

County Court), but a research study carried out at Bristol University of recently divorced people in different parts of the South West showed that 39 per cent of respondents who have children would have preferred to continue their marriage.[5]

Non-acquiescing respondents are generally discouraged by their solicitors from 'fighting' the divorce, and their anger over the allegations in the petition (38 per cent of petitions cite 'unreasonable behaviour') may be vented in destructive battles over children and money. If solicitors take up an adversarial stance on behalf of their client, conflicts may be bitter and prolonged, and the dissolution of the marriage may become the dissolution of the family. Many solicitors now favour a conciliatory approach, but a system of separate legal advice and representation increases the distance between estranged couples. Misunderstandings may be perpetuated and alternative options concerning the marriage or family arrangements may never be explored, because of the lack of communication between the couple concerned.

Conciliation and marital breakdown

Breakdown in communication seems to be the most common feature of marital breakdown. There may have been a long history of failed communication in the marriage or communication may break down in the stress of separation. Couples may withdraw from each other and stop communicating altogether, or conflict may be open and violent. As the crisis escalates, legal remedies may be sought, discarded and re-sought in a frantic search for solutions to apparently insoluble problems. In the last four years, the number of injunctions in matrimonial proceedings has risen from 12,000 to 22,000.[6] The cost of injunctions is very high (over £400 on average) and about one-third of the emergency legal aid certificates issued for injunction proceedings are abandoned, with the possibility of further application being made.

In the crisis of actual or threatened separation, individuals feel very vulnerable, angry, and deeply hurt. They may fear the loss of their children and home, as well as the loss of the marriage. If these feelings are intense, it may be impossible for them to sit down on their own in calm, rational discussion about present and future arrangements for themselves and their children. On the other hand, they may be well aware that a continuing deadlock solves nothing and may cause further harm.

Decisions taken at the time of separation may be hasty, ill-informed decisions. Nevertheless, they tend to harden into permanent arrangements which, later on, the court can do little other than approve.

The court upholds the 'status quo' unless there are very strong reasons for changing it. A study of contested custody cases in 10 courts in England and Wales showed that nearly one-third took over a year to reach a judicial decision.[7] In only two per cent of cases was the residential status quo of a child different after conclusion of the proceedings from that at the time of the petition. And in only 0.9 per cent of the total was the change brought about by a court order. The researchers commented on 'the limited effect that legal proceedings can have in these complex emotional and social conditions' and urged that procedures should be adapted to 'the urgency of these situations in recognition of the importance of their resolution in the interests of the children concerned'.

The growth of specialist conciliation services in different parts of the country shows the widespread recognition of the need for constructive methods of resolving family conflicts, which give earlier and higher priority to the needs of the children involved, and which encourage responsible decision-making by both parents. Conciliation is concerned with the acute, decision-making phase of separation and divorce, and can buttress a family in a particular stressful period of transition. It can aid the process of adjustment, but individual adjustment may take years, and some individuals will also need pre-divorce or post-divorce counselling, psychotherapy or the support and practical information provided by self-help groups such as Gingerbread and Families Need Fathers.

Conciliation may be defined as 'helping separating or divorcing couples to resolve disputes and reach agreed decisions on matters arising from the breakdown of their marriage or relationship, especially matters involving children'. Its main components are the simultaneous involvement of both partners or ex-partners in informal discussion, the neutral ground where these discussions take place, the assistance of conciliators who have specialist knowledge, experience and skills, and the integration of conciliation with legal advice and court procedures. Conciliation needs to be available before a divorce petition is filed, as well as afterwards, and should be quickly accessible in crisis situations. Referrals may be made by solicitors or the courts, with the consent of both parties, and people also need to be able to refer themselves directly, by telephoning or calling in to arrange appointments. Many referrals may be received via the Citizens Advice Bureau or other social workers, health visitors or doctors.

Training for conciliation

We have found in Bristol that conciliators need to have relevant qualifications and considerable previous experience in marital and family work, and that they need further training for conciliation itself. The work involves identifying disputed issues, helping couples to rank these issues in the order of their urgency or priority, clarifying their options and helping couples to maintain their parental role while disengaging from the failed marital relationship. It is difficult and demanding work, requiring knowledge of the law and of court procedures, understanding of the ways in which children at different stages of development react to conflict or loss, and the ability to hold angry and distressed adults while they work out their decisions. The work is concentrated and intensive, and touches deeper levels of pain and readjustment than may be apparent in agreements about access arrangements.

Conciliation is not a substitute for legal advice. The roles of the solicitor and the conciliator are complementary, and their differing knowledge and expertise may be needed to help resolve complicated interrelated issues over children, money and property. As a Canadian professor of law has observed, 'no single discipline has the omniscience which we all seek in the constructive settlement of family disputes'.[8] During 1981 Bristol Courts Family Conciliation

Service liaised with 112 firms of solicitors regarding more than 300 matrimonial cases. Two solicitors are normally involved in each case.

The organisation of conciliation services

Conciliation is developing as an interdisciplinary initiative taken in different parts of the country by senior lawyers, probation officers and others. The support of the judiciary is most important, and in a number of areas, including Bristol, conciliation management committees are chaired by local circuit judges. The probation and after-care service needs to be directly involved, to help co-ordinate pre-court and in-court services, and to safeguard standards of practice.

The creation of an expanded Civil Division of the Probation Service, responsible for both statutory divorce court welfare work and for promoting separately run conciliation services, may be a necessary and logical development. Attaching voluntary workers to heavily burdened divorce court welfare officers is inlikely to be an adequate means of handling the potential flow of urgent referrals.

An interdepartmental committee of senior officials from the Lord Chancellor's Department, the Home Office, the Department of Health and Social Security, the Central Policy Review Staff and the Treasury has been set up recently to report to ministers on the scope and effectiveness of conciliation services. The report of this committee is due by January 1983.

Results of conciliation

Conciliation is not a universal panacea, but research findings show that agreements are reached in a substantial proportion of cases, especially if conciliation is sought as the first resort, and not as a last-ditch attempt.[9] Only 19 per cent of a sample of 98 cases referred to BCFCS proceeded to contested court hearings on the issues referred for conciliation. Many custody disputes were resolved, and there was agreement or progress in 80 per cent of access disputes. Solicitors who took part in the research judged that there were actual savings in legal aid expenditure in 71 per cent of the cases in which agreements were reached, and possible savings in 96 per cent.

The Law Commission report on the financial consequences of divorce urged recently that 'everything possible should be done to encourage recourse to conciliation instead of litigation'.[10] The Lord Chancellor's Advisory Committee on Legal Aid has drawn attention to the implications of conciliation in their last four annual reports. Their latest report, for 1980-81,[11] states: 'we have heard conciliation services described as the most important development in the matrimonial field in recent years. We agree with this view and consider a decision is long overdue on how such initiatives should be directed and funded.'

It is not a question of whether we can afford conciliation services. We cannot afford not to have them. The overall net cost of civil legal aid rose by 35 per cent in 1980-81, to £35.3 million, and continued to rise in 1981-82. The recently published Government white paper on expenditure plans predicts that civil legal aid expenditure will increase by another 30 per cent in 1982-83. If it reaches the predicted total bill of £61.6 million (net cost) in 1982-83, this would make 'a staggering 73 per cent increase over two years'.[12] Two-thirds of civil legal aid expenditure is on matrimonial proceedings, and legal aid costs do not include the costs of court administration and judges' time.

The personal, social and financial costs of marriage breakdown and divorce are higher than they need be. The price is paid in terms of the distress of the families concerned, and also financially in personal and public expenditure. Conciliation, undertaken as a specialist structured task, can help to fill a major gap in statutory and voluntary services for the family and encourage much needed changes in the legal process.

References

1 Central Statistical Office: *Social Trends,* no 12, HMSO, 1981

2 Burgoyne, J and Clark, D: 'Starting again? Problems and expectations in re-marriage' in *Marriage Guidance,* vol 19, no 7, pp 334-346

3 Rimmer, L: *Families in Focus: Marriage, divorce and family patterns,* Study Commission on the Family, 1981

4 Wallerstein, JS and Kelly, JB: *Surviving the Break up: How children and parents cope with divorce,* Grant McIntyre, 1980

5 'Special procedure in divorce': research project under Mervyn Murch, Department of Social Administration, University of Bristol.

6 Law Society figures

7 Eekelar, J and Clive, E: *Custody after Divorce,* Oxford: Centre for Socio-Legal Studies, Wolfson College, 1977

8 Payne, JD: Unpublished paper

9 Research on BCFCS by Gwynn Davis, Department of Social Administration, University of Bristol

10 Law Commission: *Family Law: The consequences of divorce,* HMSO, 1981

11 Lord Chancellor's Advisory Committee on Legal Aid: *Legal Aid Annual Report* (1980/81), HMSO, 1982

12 Merricks, W: 'Government Spending: The law and order budget', *New Law Journal,* vol 132, 6044, 279-280

This article first appeared in *Concern,* published by the National Childrens' Bureau

Discussion

Nick Tyndall, in his concluding remarks, talked of the importance of taking old themes and ideas and making modern sense of them. What we were trying to do was take 'marriage' and find ways of assimilating and using the changes and choices which have become associated with it in our society. To look at change in marriage is a reaffirmation of the importance of marriage.

But, as Jackie Burgoyne pointed out, marriage does not necessarily equal happiness or divorce unhappiness—there is no blueprint for success, however you would define it, in marriage. Couples who go to the Bristol Courts Family Conciliation Service want to work out the best arrangements for their children regarding custody and access, and are actually trying to make a success of ending a marriage.

The range of choices facing individuals and couples in their personal relationships has implications for education. There must be some educational context for the exercise of choice. In talking about sex education the importance of giving information in a context of love, relationships, and trust was emphasised. But this has a wider validity, and could be applied to all education in life skills, personal relationships, marriage and parenthood. People need to be able to talk personally and privately, and this can be in families, wider kinship groups, and peer groups as well as more formal educational settings.

Jackie Burgoyne was talking about 'private lives'—about marriage as a relationship which helps individuals to find their own identity. The acceptance of the self as imperfect and the ability to disagree and criticise within a marriage are vital to the well-being of that private life.

But individuals cannot be contained entirely in one single relationship, and after talking about wider kinship and friendship from the perspective of a woman, she posed the question 'what about men?'

Unanswerable, or at any rate, unanswered, but a challenge partially taken up by Nicholas Tyndall who would like to see more discussion going on among, and about, men. Consciousness raising about men in all their roles, but particularly as husbands, fathers and family men.

The co-operation of professionals and an eclectic approach, as advocated by William Parry-Jones, is the way to try to make sense of the implications of change for those who work with marriage and families. The Bristol Courts Family Conciliation Service is the result of just such a collective effort and the study day should be a pointer towards further long-term co-operative groups.

Belfast, 2 June 1982:

Young Marriages—Who Cares?

Chairman *Terry Carlin,* Northern Ireland Officer, Irish Congress of Trade Unions.

Speakers *Nicholas Tyndall, BA,* Chief Officer, The National Marriage Guidance Council.

Louanne Hempton, BSSc, CQSW, Senior Social Worker, South Belfast Social Services, Eastern Health & Social Services Board.

Introduction

The emphasis of the Chairman, Terry Carlin of the Northern Ireland Congress of Trade Unions, in introducing the theme 'Young Marriages— Who Cares?' was on marriage being seen in a historical and social context. Marriage—affected by internal, emotional factors, but also by external pressures such as unemployment, housing and finance. As a trade union official, he had seen how stress, including marital stress, can affect people in their public capacity at work, causing accidents, injury and even death.

Thus, marriage, and the problems of young marriages today, are not just the concern of the individuals and the 'helping' agencies, but of everyone. As Roy Simpson, Chief Officer of the Northern Ireland Marriage Guidance Council, then said, we must not become 'the helpers'—'the professional'— apart from all 'the people' we work with. Helpers are people too.

Two papers were given during the day. Nicholas Tyndall used local marriage guidance council study findings to illustrate how social change is affecting young people getting married.

Louanne Hempton, using her experience as a social worker in Belfast, tried to identify the factors which may have a bearing on the breakdown of young marriages, and how separation affects the couple and their children.

Nicholas Tyndall

Marriage—a Search for Identity in an Uncertain World

Over the last two decades the National Marriage Guidance Council has concentrated on extending and improving its services as an agency. We have expanded greatly the scope of its counselling and have pioneered educational activities aimed at strengthening family life and encouraging individuals and couples to develop their potential. Most of this work has been focused on marital relationships, because of our belief that marriage in most families is the key relationship on which the health and strength of the family members are heavily dependent.

More recently, however, we have become aware of major changes in attitudes about, and behaviour within, marriage. We have been forced to pay attention to the nature of contemporary marriage, and to supplement our educational and counselling service by research into the changes taking place in what we still believe is this key relationship. The series of six study days, of which this is the fourth, are the conclusion of a year's study by MGCs into aspects of marriage which strike them, in their various parts of the country, as of particular contemporary relevance. We are here aiming to share with a wider audience the clues we have gained about the sort of changes taking place, the expectations that young people have, the gap between those and the reality they experience in their marriages, and what can best be done by helping agencies to bridge the gap.

In the course of one generation we have experienced massive changes in pressures on the family. There is no point in wasting time deciding whether these changes have been for better or for worse: generally it is for a bit of both, and those who look back nostalgically to the good old days tend to be selective in their memory about them, conveniently expunging the bad memories. There is certainly no going back on, for instance, the change brought about by technology—the enormous significance of artificial methods of contraception, including sterilisation, which have given couples considerable control over their fertility, and the all-pervading influence of the media relaying into the home challenges to parental standards and attractive presentations of alternative lifestyles.

We have witnessed also, more perhaps in England than in Ireland, sustained questioning of the authority of church and state, and of their traditional institutions of which marriage is a basic one. In England the divorce rate has quadrupled over the last 15 years, and is still rising. In Northern Ireland, where changes in the divorce law have followed about 10 years later, the divorce rate has doubled in the last three years. Whether these trends are comparable in view of the disparity in volume (in England 140,000, in Northern Ireland less than 1,000) it is clear that divorce is now a much more common factor of any social scene.

Traditional roles within the family have also been challenged on an unprecedented scale. Women have suddenly become much more articulate in complaining about their domestic lot, claiming equality and seeking choices as between home making, motherhood and career. The women's struggle to extend their perspectives has given rise to consciousness-raising groups, a phrase which signifies the search for a new identity in a changing world. And in some countries men are now beginning to respond by setting up their own groups to explore male identity—though at present such groups are mainly limited to men with a grievance related to, say, deprivation from their children through divorce or to unemployment.

Unemployment with its new and rising proportions has itself added another major pressure on many families, producing a threat to the role of the main breadwinner (generally the husband) and undermining his self-esteem in ways which do not encourage him to gain more satisfactions from greater involvement in the home. And ironically, certainly in England, while male unemployment grows, the percentage of women working increases.

Looking at marriage at the beginning of the 1980s we are therefore faced with a paradox. With a background of the continual process of urbanisation and increasing social mobility, we have experienced these economic and domestic changes, yet we have not adjusted our institutions nor our way of thinking accordingly. The choice facing young people is still either to stay single or to enter life-long marriage.

The 'official' choice is therefore a stark one, marriage identified with traditional concepts of permanence, commitment and fidelity, or singlehood. In practice other lifestyles are becoming more common, perhaps more so in England than in Northern Ireland if the percentage of marriages solemnised in church as against registry offices is anything of a pointer—50 per cent in England, 90 per cent in Northern Ireland in 1980. 'Unofficially', this sort of domestic equivalent to the 'black economy' means that in England cohabitation is rapidly increasing, both as a prelude to marriage and as an alternative to it; that over 900,000 families have only one-parent, in total bringing up about one eighth of all children; that over a million couples terminated their marriage through divorce or annulment in the decade of the 70s, and that one third of all marriages are between couples in which at least one spouse has been married before.

It is curious that these personal life histories differ so markedly from the life-long marriage required by church and registry office. Certainly one wonders whether it would not be more honest of the policy makers and more realistic to young people to provide a range of 'official' options—allowing couples to enter a short-term but renewable contract, either for a set period or during the dependent years of child-rearing.

We are in danger of dual standards. Not only is there a gap between the ideal of life-long marriage and wholesale failure in all the developed countries to achieve it, but this creates a loss of confidence among parents and in their relationship with their children. In our new world parental authority is expected to be sensitive and informed. But where parents are confused by the changing values around them and their authority is no longer tolerated if it is imposed by force, it is small wonder that opting out on issues like pre-marital sex and adolescent friendships is prevalent by parents, and that the necessary skill and understanding is beyond the ability of many fathers and mothers.

But what is the truth about contemporary attitudes? Probably the picture is very variable, according to class, geography and wealth. What we have found in many of our studies in different parts of the country during the year is that a very traditional view of marriage still persists among young people. For instance, Swansea Marriage Guidance Council administered a questionnaire to 100 young people to test some of the previous findings in the same area by Diana Leonard published in *Sex and Generation* in 1980.[1] The Welsh youngsters still express very traditional views. Ninety four per cent of the men and 100 per cent of the women wanted to get married, more than four out of five wanted to settle in the same town as their parents, and 80 per cent of the girls and over 90 per cent of the boys wanted children.

St Albans Marriage Guidance Council collected information from three very different sort of areas, and got similar though less unanimous results—88 per cent of the girls and 76 per cent of the boys expected to get married, nine out of ten would expect their spouse to be faithful, and three-quarters of the girls and two-thirds of the boys anticipated life-long marriage. These traditional views were held in spite of experience of most of the youngsters that marriages are in practice wrecked by, in order of importance, unfaithfulness, money problems, arguments, violence and children!

Walsall Marriage Guidance Council compared the views of ethnic groups and found that for the young whites, in contrast to their elders, 'the permissive society seemed remote and living together overtly before marriage was no part of their accepted life style'; that the young West Indians 'hoped for marriage relationships which would give affection, mutual support and good humour'; and that for the young Asians 'the extended family has real meaning and the involvement of a whole range of relatives in the marriage at every stage was accepted with some equanimity.'

What emerges from many of the MGC studies are strongly held views about marriage in which romance plays a vital part, and companionship and sharing feature largely. Young couples interviewed in Cambridge gave as reasons for marrying, in order of priority—emotional security, romantic attachment, ready to settle down and sexual security. The same couples allocate clear sex role differences, with cooking and house cleaning noticeably the wife's responsibilities, car maintenance and cleaning almost totally male— with jobs more important to men and young children to women. The main area for diversity was in family finances with 38 per cent of the men claiming they managed the finances, 23 per cent of the women claiming they did and a quarter of them seeing it as a shared activity.

These romantic views were summed up by one 16-year-old girl interviewed in a comprehensive school in Bracknell: 'He makes me feel like a lady, sort of thing, you know, opens doors, passes the sugar to me first. It's really nice to be treated like *someone*—respected. Nice!' This study by Bracknell MGC concluded that, though there were differences in responses given by groups, 'Beyond the differences similarities appeared throughout the groups in particular as their adult voices found space. The similarities related to the universal struggle for independence from parents: separateness subtly influenced by culturally imposed boundaries; the style of parenting which moulded them into adaptation or rebellion; the liberating effect of accepting parents or parent substitutes, where choice without pressure to conform or reject, was nurtured.'

This study points to what seems to be as great a divide as ever, a different approach to domestic choices in adult life according to social and cultural background. The importance of good parenting has been mentioned. Educational attainment is also vital. The Swansea studies show that the majority of youngsters court between 16 and 18, marry early, settle near their parents and get little satisfaction from work. But those who achieve educationally, break out from that mould, go off to higher education, have a pattern of courtship which involves several friendships and marry in their late 20s.

The Marriage Guidance Council in Sunderland, a North East town with unemployment reaching 30 per cent, paints a similar picture of lack of opportunity among educational non-achievers in a comprehensive school. Their expectations of satisfaction in marriage were as pessimistic as their hopes of obtaining regular employment:

> Unemployment is accepted with an air of resignation because, after all, it's all caused by 'them out there'. What happens is always someone else's fault be it the neighbours, the council, the police, the government, etc . . .
>
> The same situation is mirrored in how this group view interpersonal relationships and marriage. Things that happen are external to the individual. Things happen to him and force him to behave in particular ways.

Nevertheless, a large majority expected to get married, and surprisingly, nine out of ten hoped for a church wedding.

This group had low expectations of themselves, unlike those who were successful educationally, and the only hope of moving to independence, of becoming a significant individual, seems to be in marrying or having a baby. It seems as if these youngsters are looking to marriage as their main hope in establishing their adult identity—yet, ironically, doing so at a time when the institution of marriage seems to be more fluid and less certain than ever before.

Again, paradoxically, as marriage is making more and and more demands in terms of joint decision-making, flexible roles, sexual prowess and skilled parenthood, so it is contracted early by those who have least ability or training to meet those demands.

The marriage of 'good companions' requires a high level of sensitivity and emotional security which can withstand threats to the self arising from the closeness of an intimate relationship, and a capacity to stick at it in difficult times in order to (in the jargon) 'work through' the problems—in other words to tolerate the black periods, doubts and uncertainties, and keep going in the belief that there will soon emerge some light at the end of the tunnel. Those are heavy demands, highly satisfactory when attainable but by no means always an attractive proposition when compared with the immediate satisfaction of sampling the grass in the next field!

Incidentally this search for identity becomes quickly apparent again when marriages break down. The high remarriage rate following divorce or death of one spouse (nearly 10 per cent of all marriages in Northern Ireland, though now over a third of all marriages in England and Wales) is statistical proof of the phenomenon known so well by marriage counsellors that the withdrawal of a dependent relationship through the loss of one spouse poses an identity crisis for the remaining partner which she, or particularly he, seeks to resolve by becoming intimately dependent on a new partner.

So far I have talked about marriage in its significance as a relationship between the couple. This search for closeness and mutual affirmation, however, comes under pressure when pregnancy begins, and comes emotionally, and indeed physically, between the couple. Not surprisingly more couples today are exercising their choice not to face this disruption by remaining childless, or, as it is now sometimes termed, childfree. Reading Marriage Guidance Council studied couples who had decided not to parent. From a small sample of ten couples, a clear view emerged that children would remove 'freedom'—of expression, thought and action—and that was too high a price for them to pay, even at the cost of 'missing out'. As one of the couples expressed their views:

> We observed our friends getting tied down and tired out by children and having very little time to devote to their relationship. We are worried that children could upset our relationship through: difficulty in sharing the work of caring for them, jealousies, inability to continue the life we're currently enjoying, creating noise and chaos! Also we don't see the need to have children in a world that has high unemployment and a huge nuclear war hanging over it.

The conscious choice not to have children is still very much a minority one, however, and it is entirely different from those couples who want children but are infertile, and, alas, nowadays are faced with a shortage of adoptive children. The latter situation causes great anguish and, not surprisingly, self-help groups have emerged to provide support for such couples.

For those with children, there is not just the additional financial and physical demands, which are well known, but there are also subtle psychological factors to do with disruption of the 'ideal' twosome relationship. Jersey Marriage Guidance Council in their study 'On Being Three' concluded that pregnancy and birth remains predominantly a mother's world, in spite of the fact that 70 per cent of fathers now attend the birth of their baby and all the emphasis on sharing. Their conclusion sounds an ominous note:

> While the services concerned with babies may provide adult companionship and reassurance on aspects of child behaviour, they may not be effective in providing support to the marriage. How to bring fathers in on the act is the problem.

Difficulties connected with the arrival of children also featured prominently in a study undertaken by Dorset Marriage Guidance Council. They asked 75 couples in stable marriages what events in the life cycle had caused most problems. Top of the list came the birth of the first child (38 per cent), next came the birth of subsequent children (28 per cent), with relationships with dependent parents coming third (19 per cent).

It would be wrong to present the arrival of children solely as a source of tensions. The Cambridge Marriage Guidance Council survey demonstrates most vividly the two sides of the coin—for heading the list of 'difficulties' facing their respondents came 'children' (with 'money' as a close second), but top also of the 'rewards' came 'children' scored by 47 out of the 52 couples. The survey concludes that 'the advent of children to a pair is easily the most significantly disturbing event . . . which complicates their emphasis on the joys of belonging/togetherness, and the difficulty of maintaining these alongside the individuality and separateness of the self.'

The helping services need great understanding of these internal pressures on the couple, especially of the emotional challenge to fathers as they experience the intimacy of their marital relationship taking second place to the intimacy of their wife's relationship with the new baby. It may be that medical and social services are good at giving an affirmative answer to the question 'who cares?' when it is posed in terms of mother and baby care, but the answer is much less certain when the question refers to father and the couple's relationship.

Concluding comments

I am aware that I have talked about young marriages in terms of marriage *relationships*. I have not talked about the practical issues facing young families, because I have left that to Louanne Hempton who has day-to-day knowledge of the situation in the Province. Northern Ireland comes way down the UK tables on all factors such as housing and poverty, so clearly a great number of the problems associated with family life here must be attributable to lack of adequate conditions in which to live and raise children satisfactorily.

I do not minimise these issues, and I know I would be financially and emotionally unable to manage to tolerate a family of three or four children on a low wage in cramped conditions. Families in such conditions are familiar not only to social services but also to local authority representatives, trade union officials, clergy and MPs. The pressure at such points of contact is always to provide amelioration of the environment, and that is entirely understandable.

Nevertheless marital satisfaction depends to a greater or lesser degree on interaction between external practical factors and internal feelings and self-expression. If we fall into the temptation of ascribing all difficulties to environmental factors, we miss the changes that are taking place in relationships, particularly in those classes of society who are not bowed down by poverty and inadequate housing. Helping services need to campaign for better living conditions. But in their work, whether in schools, communities and parishes, health centres or social services, they also need to be aware of the transitions that are happening in family relationships, which are experienced by some as highly disruptive, but which are used by others as opportunities in the search for personal identity in an uncertain world.

References

1 Leonard, D: *Sex and Generation: A study of courtship and weddings,* Tavistock, 1980

Louanne Hempton

The Breakdown of Young Marriages

D r Johnson's famous quips that the 'popularity of marriage is a triumph of hope over experience', and 'that marriage has many pains but celibacy has few pleasures', illustrate two central facts about modern marriage. Marriage as an institution has never been more popular, yet divorce rates have never been higher especially in young marriages.

The purpose of this paper is, therefore, to investigate this problem under four basic headings. Firstly, the factors which influence the breakdown of marriage; secondly, the problems which occur when marriages are not working properly; thirdly, the difficulties involved in separation and after; and finally to pose the question—where do we go from here?

In doing so I will be speaking as a senior social worker based in a busy inner city social service department. The thrust of the paper will therefore not be academic or statistical but rather practical and experiential. Moreover, because the problem under investigation is so enormously complicated, a social work perspective is only one of many. Equally valuable are your contributions, whatever your background—clerical, domestic or professional. The more light shed on these matters, the better.

Broadly speaking, then, the people with marital problems who come to the attention of social services departments do so in three different ways:

a Those who refer themselves because they are experiencing problems in their marriage. Frequently in these cases only one partner, usually the wife, approaches the department, either personally or through an outside body, e.g. a health visitor, a GP, or a friend.

b Those who are referred, or refer themselves, for a completely different reason, but where it later transpires that marital problems are pertinent to the difficulties being experienced.

Initial reasons for referral can vary from a simple enquiry about benefits to possible child abuse, and often include problems about housing, depression, inability to organise the home, or difficulties with the children.

c Those who are referred by the court under the Matrimonial Causes Order 1978 or the Domestic Proceedings Order 1980.

It is from these three groups that most of my information will be drawn. Throughout the paper, most of the statistics and examples will be from Northern Ireland, with additional information from Britain and Europe.

Factors influencing the breakdown of marriage

While it has been said that marriage has never been so popular (we do not need to look for evidence of this, new bridal shops are regularly being opened, glossy bridal magazines abound, and surveys show that more and more young people want to get married), divorce and separation figures are rising.

We are all familiar with statements like:

'At the present rate one in three marriages is heading for divorce.'

'One in four of all children will during its childhood live with a person who is not its natural parent.'

'The cost to the tax-payer of legal aid for separation and divorce is approximately £40 million a year and rising.'

'In 1980 there were estimated to be 920,000 one parent families in Great Britain (approximately one in eight). This cost approximately £300 million in benefits. Children in care cost a further £230 million.'

'In Northern Ireland, the number of divorces in 1977 was approximately 700. Last year it was approximately 1600. Of these 1600, approximately 1000 had children under 18 years of age, and of those 1000, approximately 500 occurred in the Eastern Board Area.'

Yet no-one believes it will ever happen to them. What, therefore, are the factors which influence the breakdown of marriage?

Fundamental changes in social structures and attitudes

It is not enough to investigate the reasons for marital breakdown purely within the narrow confines of a single relationship. It is now clear that a whole series of changes in 20th century Western society have imposed new strains on marital stability. They include:

The breakdown of traditional reinforcements of social conformity
This includes community fragmentation due to larger towns, economic individualism, and increased mobility; the reduction of ecclesiastical influence due to secularisation; reduced influence of the extended and more recently the nuclear family and the increase of peer group influence.

Significantly, these processes have been slower in Northern Ireland where divorce and separation rates are still lower than in the rest of Britain.

Changing courtship patterns
Edward Shorter, in his book *The Making of the Modern Family,*[1] argues that with the reduction of parental and community control, courtship has become more anonymous. He states that 'Several large scale studies have inquired where the spouses met. In Sweden, for example, one third had met at dances. In France almost one half—more so among young couples—had encountered each other in such anonymous situations as movies, dances, vacation trips or just in the street.'

Higher expectations of marriage

The cumulative influence of mass education, television, films, magazines, novels and popular music has persuaded a whole generation that the marital relationship should fulfil a wide range of expectations—romance, sexual satisfaction, companionship, self-fulfilment, and more or less a continuous happiness. This is in marked contrast to the predominantly economic motive and child-bearing function of marriage in earlier historical periods.

Intensification of couples' erotic life

Major investigations into sexual behaviour have revealed dramatic changes in the past 20 years. The increased availability of contraception has had a significant effect on young people's attitudes towards sexual relationships; most young people now have important sexual experiences before marriage; women have developed higher expectations of sexual relationships; and whereas in traditional societies sexuality mainly served an instrumental purpose, it is now seen as an important end in itself.

Shorter concludes a stimulating chapter on these changes by stating that growing eroticism 'has injected a huge chunk of high explosive into a couple's relationship. Because sexual attachment is notoriously unstable, couples resting atop such a base may easily be blown apart'.

The changing role of women

It is difficult to talk in general terms about this because there are so many variables to be taken into account, e.g. social class, urban or rural areas, working or non working women etc. One can state with some certainty, however, that the percentage of working women has increased, and that women who become more economically independent are also more likely to pull out of unsatisfactory marriages. Moreover, the State's financial contribution to the separated woman and her family has provided a degree of economic independence, previously unobtainable for the majority of women.

In broader terms the emphasis placed on women's liberation has necessitated difficult new adjustments within marital roles. Many males, with traditional values, have found this threatening, confusing and annoying.

Yet while general social trends tell us a good deal about the pressures with which individuals have to cope, in the last analysis, our concern has to be with particular relationships. The reasons for marital breakdown in the cases that come to our attention may be conveniently divided into two categories, primary and secondary factors affecting the marriage relationship.

Primary factors affecting the marriage relationship include: the couple's expectations; the reason for marriage—e.g. romance, escape, love, duty, pregnancy; each partner's initial commitment to the marriage compared with commitment to peer group, family, work, hobbies; the couple's family background and the level of support available; the degree to which the couple share beliefs and culture; the age and maturity of the couple at the time of marriage.

On this last point—in Northern Ireland, in 50 per cent of all divorces where children were involved, one of the partners was under 20 at the time of marriage. While in England and Wales the age at marriage is rising, in Northern Ireland the trend would seem to be towards younger marriages.

However mature the couple may be when they enter marriage, unfavourable circumstances can impose serious strains on a relationship, and these are what I have called the secondary factors which may affect marriage. Inadequate housing, shoestring budgets, unemployment (or the high demands of some kinds of employment), alcohol abuse, gambling, political unrest, pressure from children and the poor physical and mental health of each partner, can slowly but inexorably undermine young relationships.

Bearing in mind all these points, in our experience there are also times when marriages appear to be particularly vulnerable to stress. Critical points include the first two years, the birth of a child (or in some cases pregnancy itself), the loss of work, a move of home or bereavement in the family.

Problems when marriages are not working properly

Despite these pressures and the apparent increase in the rate of breakdown, the transition from the optimistic marriage ceremony to the pessimistic court case is not normally an easy journey—people often remain together even when there are serious difficulties in their relationship.

This brings us to a point which is controversial but which nevertheless has to be faced. While there may be little argument that a husband and wife are happiest when their relationship is based on love and mutual trust and where there is a real desire to encourage the other person to develop to the best of his/her ability, and while we may agree that a child does best in a home where there are two people who care for him and each other, I wonder how often this ideal occurs in our society? Even in the strongest and healthiest of marriages there are times when adjustment is required, when difficulties arise and when problems need to be faced.

In many cases this happens either through the family's use of its own resources or through help from an outsider. In an increasing number, however, this cannot be said to be the case. While many marriages can adapt, mature and develop through their difficulties, in others the problems, even after help and counselling, seem to be insurmountable.

What happens, then, in a marriage where apparently only one partner is committed to working at the difficulties, where communication between the partners has broken down, where, in maturing, the partners have 'grown away' from each other, where there is a feeling of real hostility and resentment, or where neither partner's emotional needs are being met within the marriage? Should these marriages be encouraged to continue or should they end?

Sadly, from the experience of the cases that come to our attention, (which are often extreme but not necessarily unrepresentative of wide social patterns), unhappy marriages have a profoundly detrimental effect on those involved. These effects vary greatly but the most common are:

- loss of esteem by one or both partners—this can lead to depression, attention seeking behaviour, illness, use of drugs, nagging and withdrawal.
- solace being sought outside the marriage, e.g. through sport, other relationships, drinking, gambling, work
- distorted communication

- hostility, possibly leading to violence, both physical and verbal
- child neglect and abuse (in the very broadest of terms)
- behavioural difficulties with children—they become more withdrawn, do not reach their full potential, bed-wet, show signs of illness, (often psychosomatic—stomach pains, nightmares, headaches), they play one parent off against the other. Truancy and p.oblems in school increase, and occasionally they run away from home.

To sum up then, what I am arguing is that extremely bad marriages pose as many serious problems as separation itself.

The difficulties of separation

While unhappy marriages produce depressing results, separation itself creates a whole set of new problems. The point of separation is never easy, and even the most amicable of arrangements are usually characterised by practical and emotional problems.

On the emotional level, the actual feelings which occur around the time of separation are often very confused and difficult to sort out. Frequently this makes decision making hard and commitment to the future difficult. People's reactions vary greatly, but the most common are:

- depression, with a resultant inability to organise one's life
- overwhelming anger and resentment
- shame
- a crushing sense of failure
- loss of esteem and belief in oneself
- numbness
- fear
- guilt
- confusion
- ambivalence
- hopelessness
- relief.

Often the act of leaving the home causes a reaction of repentance, which may or may not lead to a positive readjustment in the relationship. In the kind of society we have, which is still orientated towards couples, it is not surprising that the loss of wife/husband status and loneliness sometimes result in temporary or permanent reunions. But, it must be said that frequent separations and reunions only increase the emotional damage to all concerned, including the children. Moreover, the emotional problems of separation need to be carefully worked through. If this is not done children may be caught between separated, but still hostile parents. An additional reason for tackling the emotional problems of separation is to prevent the formation of further destructive relationships. For example, it is often the case that battered wives are drawn into another violent relationship because of unresolved feelings of worthlessness.

In the midst of these emotional entanglements, children need special protection. Imagine how a child feels when he is continually told that his father is all bad or when he sees his mother being beaten by another man. It is scarcely surprising that children subjected to such experiences are themselves much more likely to be involved in violent and unhappy relationships later in life. In this respect at least the 'sins' of parents are indeed visited on their children.

On a more pragmatic level, separation poses serious problems which are worth investigating in some detail.

What to do next
Despite all the publicity about separation, most people who think about leaving home have little idea how to go about it. They are often bewildered by the practical tasks facing them. They have to fight their way through various different organisations to establish themselves as independent units at precisely the time when they are most emotionally vulnerable. They need simple factual advice and practical support. For example, someone to look after the children while they enquire about benefits, see solicitors etc. This kind of advice and support is often not as readily available as it might be.

Accommodation
Obviously if a couple are to separate they cannot live under the same roof —someone has to move out. Sometimes this can be agreed amicably, but often it cannot. In such cases major upheaval is inevitable. It is true that under the domestic proceedings legislation an exclusion and protection order can be granted by which a husband can be removed from the marital home if the threat of violence can be proved. Most frequently, however, it is still the wife and children who leave the home—she may not have sufficient grounds for an exclusion order; she may live in an area where it cannot be enforced; or she may feel unable to stay in the home.

In these circumstances alternative accommodation has to be found for the wife and children. If they are unable to afford rented accommodation then they will have to move in with family, friends or even a hostel, pending the separation and decisions about housing. This difficult situation may continue for many months, and when a family is eventually rehoused, it is often in a new neighbourhood, where friends and supports are limited.

Finance
Although in many cases the financial arrangements are satisfactorily worked out, frustration can arise when people have to adjust to a lower income or to life on supplementary benefit. Whereas before the separation a salary only had to pay for one house, two premises now have to be financed. It is well known that maintenance payments can be a source of animosity.

The legal system
Despite recent changes, marital law is still based on a judicial system which has as its basis the traditional adversarial model of the British legal code. This means that legal representatives are called upon to represent the interests of their client rather than corporate concerns of all the parties. The process itself often takes place in what appears to be a very public, foreboding building, and there is often insufficient time available to thrash out the recurring and often highly complicated issues of access and property.

Thus, the very legal processes laid down to resolve problems can themselves create new pain and bitterness. On a popular level, the film *Kramer Versus Kramer* clearly demonstrated how the need for tasty evidence can undermine the basic human dignity which the legal system prides itself on protecting. Of course no legal system can fully take into account the emotional complexities of separation cases, but we must continually review the machinery to make sure that it is as human as possible.

However, let us not get the situation totally out of perspective. In looking at the divorces which took place in the Eastern Board in 1981, a number of points are worthy of note.

In the majority of cases, both parents and children stated that existing arrangements were the best that could be achieved under the circumstances and that they had been able to adjust to the marriage breakdown.

In many cases, (particularly those where there had been a high level of tension and violence in the marriage) the children were often more settled after the parents had separated than they had been before. This improvement is, however, related to how far the parents were able to come to terms with the separation.

There was a correlation between the age at separation and the degree of subsequent adjustment. Younger parents and children were able to adjust to marital breakdown more easily. In Northern Ireland fewer fathers had, or expected to have, access to their children, than in Great Britain. Where difficulties did occur, however, they were frequently in this area. In cases where access occurred, and where a partner subsequently remarried, the child's ability to accept the situation was affected by his preparation for the marriage and the other parent's acceptance of the marriage.

Finally, then, where do we go from here? This of course, is the most difficult question of all. Complicated problems, as Garrett Fitzgerald has recently reminded us, do not have easy solutions. All I can hope to do is to state some of the key issues as a stimulus to further discussion.

Despite all the difficulties mentioned earlier people still want to get married; most people stay married; and those who separate, frequently get remarried. Dr Johnson is right, marriage does have many pains but it seems that celibacy has few pleasures! How then can we build on this? Do we, for example, need to give more attention to pre-marriage guidance? How can we educate people about the realities of marriage? How can we more effectively help those who are experiencing problems?

In facing up to marital breakdown, there are two quite different, but by no means mutually exclusive strategies. Either we can try to ease those problems which increase marital instability, whilst admitting that some factors are more within our control than others. For example it may be possible to ameliorate housing, financial and employment difficulties, but how far can we change social structures and attitudes? Or we can accept that society has irrevocably changed and that marital breakdown will inevitably continue at high levels. That being the case, should we then work for a more humane separation process in the interests of all concerned? What would be the future effects for our society, and for our children, in pursuing either of these courses?

References

1   Shorter, E: *The Making of the Modern Family,* Fontana, 1977

Discussion

Discussion throughout the day had three threads running through it: the expectations young people today have of marriage; the disparity of their conscious and unconscious expectations; and the question of education for marriage and personal relationships.

Young people may have more invested in marriage and their dreams of marriage than ever before. Society—and particularly the media—transmits conflicting pictures and values, with traditional sex roles contrasted with more recent notions of sharing and equality. The propaganda about the joys of being in love, married, a mother and a perfect homemaker, contrasted with media coverage of divorce, family violence, and unhappiness.

The media have a valuable role in sharing the realities of life with people and letting them know they are not alone in what they experience. But there is a tendency for the media, advertising, and many other institutions, to bolster people's expectations of marriage and married life to a quite unrealistic extent. Although this idealistic view of marriage may be nurtured more in urban than rural areas, for many people everywhere marriage has magical qualities and will cure all ills.

So marriage may be seen as a panacea by those looking towards it. Once married couples have to try to realise these expectations, and the premium currently put on achieving 'success'—in marriage, in sex, at work and socially—makes the goals even more difficult, or impossible, to achieve.

In talking about expectations of marriage, it was suggested that a distinction should be made between conscious and unconscious reasons for getting married. The conscious reasons that a couple give—sociological, religious or financial—may hide an unconscious but very real desire for developing intimacy in the privacy of a marriage relationship. Marriage preparation should then be trying to raise these unconscious wishes to consciousness.

Participants stressed the importance of framing discussion with young people in terms of their current experience of relationships. Education work can be very useful if it starts at the point at which young people have arrived and therefore is not all hypothetical. Finally, on education, why is it always thought that the need for education stops at marriage, or at the birth of the first child? Considering the difficulties that many couples experience in their early years of marriage and especially after the birth of their first child, post marriage education could be recommended, with baptism as a possible point at which contacts could be made.

Just before the final plenary the participants split into four groups, and each one came up with a key point relating to the title of their group.

The group looking at the structure of marriage suggested that couples might have some kind of marital review every so often. The education work discussion group called for a centre to collect and disseminate information and relevant experience. The third group was looking at the role of counsellor and helper in relation to young marriages, and they posed the question—how do you get to the families who may need help?

The final group included the two speakers and the chairman, and the thought this group was left with was—casework or community change? Do the 'helpers' deal with what comes to their doors, or do they involve themselves in the politics of social change? If so, how?

Nicholas Tyndall suggested that marriage guidance councils embody the community's care for marriage, by acting on behalf of communities in caring for their marriages. But, going back to Roy Simpson's opening remarks, the 'community's carers' must not get too remote from the people to whom they belong.

Newcastle-upon-Tyne, 30 June 1982:

Changing Patterns of Marriage and Remarriage

Chairman   *Jonathan Brown,* Senior Counsellor, Open University (Northern Region).

Speakers   *Lesley Rimmer, MSc,* Research Officer, Study Commission on the Family. Author of *Families in Focus.* Formerly a Senior Lecturer in Economics, Polytechnic of the South Bank.

              David Clark, MRC Medical Sociology Unit, Aberdeen. Special research interests—second marriages and step-parenting.

Introduction

'Current discussions about the family—and the controversies they can generate—depend crucially on interpretations about how family patterns and family life are changing. Certainly changes are taking place, but how significant are they?'

(Lesley Rimmer, *Families in Focus*)

Lesley Rimmer, research officer of the Study Commission on the Family, started the day talking about the changes which have occurred in marriage, divorce, and remarriage as shown in national statistics. This approach provided the basic data from which to start to understand the implications for individuals, and for the wider field of public and social policy.

David Clark, from the MRC Medical Sociology Unit in Aberdeen, followed with a paper based on the results of some intensive work done with newly-wed couples, some marrying for the first time and others remarrying. He outlined couples' feelings about marriage and their expectations of marriage, and remarked on the lack of difference between first time newlyweds and remarried newlyweds in this respect.

Lesley Rimmer

Changing Patterns of Marriage and Remarriage

The ways in which marriage and remarriage are changing is a vast and complex subject about which one must be selective. In this paper I focus on those aspects of three major issues—marriage, divorce and remarriage— which are most potentially significant in affecting the experience and meaning of marriage. And it is important to stress that these issues are not just a private concern of the individuals involved but have a number of important implications for public policy. Much of the work of the Study Commission on the Family has focused on these issues.

First then, let us consider the way in which patterns of marriage have been changing. Marriage is still a very popular institution: nearly nine out of ten people will marry at some stage in their lives and this is a higher level than at earlier periods. First marriage rates—that is the number of marriages per thousand single people—reached a peak in the late 1960s and early 1970s and have been falling since that time. And this has led to concern that in some way we were beginning to see a rejection of marriage by the young.

In fact we would be premature to jump to this conclusion: there are both 'statistical' reasons why marriage rates should have fallen after the early 1970s, in the wake of the Family Law Reform Act, and there have also been changes in the age at marriage. Indeed the long term trend to a falling age at first marriage turned round after 1971 and the median age of first marriage for both men and women is now six months higher than it was in 1971.[1] Part of the explanation of this is the increased likelihood that couples will cohabit—either as a prelude to marriage or as a 'replacement' for marriage—and cohabitation is now quite commonplace.

Around ten per cent of women who first married between 1971 and 1975 had lived with their husbands before marriage, compared with three per cent who were married for the first time five years earlier. Data from 1979 General Household Survey suggests that this proportion had risen to 20 per cent for those married in the late 1970s and, in addition, about one in ten single women aged 20-29 reported currently cohabiting.[2]

It is still too early to tell, however, what the trends in cohabitation really mean: are they seen as 'trial' marriages or as alternatives? The balance

101

of evidence suggests the former: but it is clearly an important area for further research. And we must recognise how cohabitees themselves view their situation.

In the *Family Formation* survey cohabiting women were asked whether they considered themselves 'married' or not:

> 'The answers distinguished clearly between two groups. Those who saw the relationship as a long term commitment, usually including having children and sharing possessions and income, regarded themselves as married. They frequently were unable to marry because one of them was waiting for a divorce. The second group who did not regard themselves as married were much less likely to recognise a long term commitment to their partner, did not share possessions and finances, and neither had nor planned to have children. They tended to regard their cohabitation as convenient.'[3]

In this study, three per cent of the single, widowed, divorced or separated women reported that they were cohabiting—and of these, two-fifths regarded themselves as married.

The other trend in marriage is the increasing proportion of marriages which are remarriages. Indeed only 65 per cent of all 'new' marriages are first marriages. And an increasing proportion of marriages involve partners who have both previously been divorced—and it is to marriage 'breakdown' that I now turn.

Marriage breakdown

In 1980 there were 12 divorces per thousand married couples, a total of some 148,000 divorces in all. This was *six times* the 1961 rate and *double* the rate in 1971.[4] If divorce rates continue at this level then it has been estimated recently that one in ten couples would divorce before their sixth wedding anniversary, one in five before their twelfth anniversary, and nearly one in four before they have been married for 15 years. Overall, by 35 years of marriage, one in three marriages can be expected to end in divorce.[5] These average figures, though stunning in themselves, hide a complex reality. For an individual the risk of divorce depends strongly on two factors: the age of the wife at marriage and the duration of marriage.

The younger the wife at marriage, the greater the risk of divorce, irrespective of how long the marriage has lasted. For marriages which have lasted at least three years, the divorce rate for women married in their teens is twice as high as for those who married between 20 and 24, and three times as high as for those who married between the ages of 25 and 29.

Again, for the individual, the risk of divorce within marriage is higher at some periods than at others. Although figures relating to the actual time of divorce were affected by the law governing divorce, and also do not reflect the true duration of marriage, there are some interesting differences by duration of marriage. The highest rate of divorce currently occurs three years after marriage when one couple in thirty divorces. Seven and 12 years after marriage, divorce rates have fallen to about two thirds and one half respectively of their value at three years' marriage duration, and they continue to decline the longer the duration. My interpretation of this is that the longer the marriage continues the more likely it is that it will continue. But having said that, one in 20 of all divorces in 1979 were of marriages of more than 30 years' duration.

When do people divorce: at what age and how long have they been married? During the 1970s there has been a substantial rise in the proportion of divorces occurring at short durations of marriage. In 1970, 3.9 per cent of all divorces occurred at three years' duration, and a further nine per cent at four years. In 1979 it was 8.9 per cent at three years (that is, nearly three times as great) and 8.7 per cent at four years. Indeed, nearly one in five (18.5 per cent) of all divorces in 1979 took place before the end of five years of marriage, and a further one in three (30 per cent) before ten years of marriage.

If the age at marriage and risk of divorce by duration of marriage are linked, then it is possible to estimate the age at which people are most at risk of divorce. Rates of divorce are highest between the ages of 25 and 29 when nearly one in thirty couples divorces (28 per thousand). The risk of divorce at these ages, for both men and women, is about twice the overall rate, and about six times the rate at ages over 45.

There has been, in parallel with the increasing proportion of divorces occurring early in marriage, an increase in the proportion of divorces granted to wives at younger ages. In 1974 in 11 per cent of all divorces the wife was under 25 at divorce, and in 55 per cent of the cases she was under 35. By 1980 14 per cent of wives were less than 25 at the time of their divorce, and 59 per cent under 35.[6] For divorcing couples without dependent children, the increase has been even greater, from 11 and 42 per cent in 1974 to 17 and 54 per cent in 1980 (i.e. divorcees are getting younger).

It can be seen then that during the late 1970s the proportion of all divorcing couples in which the wife was still of child bearing age has grown. This has particular implications for the likelihood of childbearing within a reconstituted family, and it is to the position of children that I now turn.

In England and Wales in 1980 60 per cent of all divorcing couples had children under 16, and a further ten per cent had children over 16.[7] So the proportion of divorces where no 'children' at all are involved is, at three in ten, very low. The proportion is, obviously, much higher at earlier durations of marriage. Seventy one per cent of divorces which took place within the first two years were of childless couples as were 66 per cent of those divorcing at three years of marriage. But by the time ten to 14 years duration of marriage is reached, only 15 per cent—one in six—of divorcing couples have, or have had, no children. This falls to just nine per cent for those who have been married 15 to 19 years.[8]

If we turn specifically to the children in divorce, then 163,221 children under 16 saw their parents divorce in 1980. Of these about a quarter were under five, just over 40 per cent were between five and ten and about one third were between 11 and 15. In 1971 only half as many children—82,000— saw their parents divorce but since the number of children per divorcing couple had stayed fairly constant the increasing numbers of children involved in divorce simply reflects the increasing number of divorces. For children, the highest risk period of being involved in divorce is between five and ten when about 16 children per thousand see their parents divorce each year, and on this basis between one in five and one in six children will see their parents divorce—at least once—before they reach 16.[9] Indeed, currently whereas 90 per cent of all children under five are living with both natural parents, this is true of only 80 per cent of children in the ten to 15 year age group.[10] Marriage breakdown, however, is not synonymous with divorce. In addition to those who divorce, at any one time, there will be others who are currently separated and will subsequently divorce, and others who will be reunited.

Separation and Divorce

It is not until recently that we have had a better idea about the extent of informal separations; but some evidence on this came from Dunnell's survey on *Family Formation 1976*—she showed that divorce statistics in the 1960s were measuring only about half the total breakdowns of marriage. Among women married between 1961 and 1965 for example, 11 per cent said they had separated by ten years after marriage compared with only six per cent who had actually divorced. Many of these women may now have divorced and remarried and it seems likely that the extent to which divorce understates marriage breakdown is less than previously. This is primarily because there has been a general tendency for women to obtain a divorce sooner after their separation.[11]

And in terms of time, the trends Dunnell analysed suggested that two-thirds of separations have resulted in divorce within four years of separation. This time is important because it affects the ability to remarry and also affects our perception of the actual duration of marriages at divorce.

Remarriage

Many people question the impact of divorce on marriage 'as an institution'. Clearly divorce can be said to represent disillusion with a particular marriage, but equally clearly it cannot be said to represent disillusion with marriage as an institution. For those under 30 at divorce, remarriage rates are high—about one third of those who divorce before they are 30 remarry each year, which means that within five years some 80 per cent will have remarried. Indeed remarriage is a growing part of all marriages. More than one in three of all 'new' marriages is a remarriage for one or other spouse and in 1980, 11.4 per cent of marriages involved both partners who had previously been divorced, and 21 per cent of *all persons* marrying had previously been divorced.[12] On present trends, it has been estimated that one person in five will have been married at least twice by the year 2000.[13]

Again, remarriage is a vast and complex subject, and I want to be selective and consider three questions: first, who remarries whom? Second, how soon do people remarry? And third, what are the major trends?

It is clear from the typology of marriage that 'like' marries 'like' more often than not: spinsters are more likely to marry bachelors and divorcees are more likely to marry divorcees. For a growing number of couples it will be marriage 'second time around' after divorce for both parties. For me, this emphasises the importance of 'civilising' the process of divorce once couples have decided that they can no longer remain married, so that they can re-enter marriage with their confidence dented as little as possible.

In fact, a surprisingly high proportion of people remarry quickly after divorce. Over one quarter of the women aged under 50 in 1979 who had been divorced, and subsequently remarried during the second half of the 1970s, remarried within three months of obtaining their divorce.[14] In the 'record linkage' study of divorce, one third of those who divorced and had remarried within four and a half years, had remarried within three months and 60 per cent within one year.[15]

Partly this reflects the Divorce Reform Act, which freed a lot of couples to remarry, but there is also a slight, although not very consistent, trend for people to form new unions faster after their separations. Cohabitation complicates the picture, and there is a much higher probability that these 'remarriages' will in fact be cohabitation than is the case with first marriages.

By four years after separation, 34 per cent of those separated between 1961 and 1965 were 'remarried'—20 per cent of that 34 per cent being legally married. The same figure was achieved by three years after separation for those separated between 1970 and 1971—but in this group those cohabiting exceeded those legally married.[16] If anything this could indicate an increased popularity of 'remarriage' in the sense of people living together, although formal remarriage *rates,* along with first marriage rates, have been declining. And the explanation is similar—the rise in cohabitation.

But do those who remarry get it right next time? A growing proportion of all divorces involve redivorce. Nearly one in ten people who divorced had been divorced before. But this partly reflects the growing number of divorcees who had remarried: as yet we cannot reliably estimate the risk of divorce for second marriages with any accuracy.

Conclusion

I have presented a very factual picture of trends in marriage, divorce and remarriage (based on data for England and Wales). I hope we will be able to flesh out the meaning of these trends in discussion, but they are of themselves quite startling:

- one in three marriages is a remarriage for one or other party
- one in three will end in divorce
- one in five people will have been married twice by the year 2000

All these trends have significant and important implications for many areas of public policy: yet changes are little understood. The work of the Study Commission on the Family has addressed this in a number of areas.

But these changes are important not just for reasons of public policy, but because they affect people's views of life and attitudes towards divorcees and people marrying again: and they must be fundamentally affecting the views people have of marriage. Whether they regard marriage as being 'for life' or as a relatively short term commitment—whether the fact that you know others who are divorced, affects your view of 'life after divorce'—or allows you to contemplate it.

Certain crucial questions are raised:

- When marriage ends does parenting also have to end?
- What effects will these levels of divorce and remarriage have on networks of social care?
- What are the implications for the social security system?

It is clear that while much is known, many of these changes have implications which require careful consideration and continual monitoring. This is the challenge that they pose, and one response is the development of a 'family perspective' on policy issues.

References

1 OPCS: *Marriages 1980,* Monitor FM2 82/2 1982, Table 5. Median ages at first marriage are 24.0 years for males and 21.8 years for females.

2 Brown, A and Kierman, K: 'Cohabitation in Great Britain', *Population Trends,* 25, OPCS/HMSO, 1981

3 Dunnell, K: *Family Formation 1976,* OPCS/HMSO, 1979

4 OPCS, *Divorces 1980,* Monitor FM2 82/1

5 Haskey, J: 'The Proportion of Marriages Ending in Divorce', *Population Trends,* 27, OPCS/HMSO, 1981

6 FM2 82/2, op cit

7 FM2 82/1, op cit

8 Ibid

9 Rimmer, L: *Families in Focus,* The Study Commission on the Family, 1981

10 OPCS: *General Household Survey 1979,* HMSO, 1981, Table 8.23

11 Dunnell, K: op cit, p 38, Table 7.7

12 FM2 82/2, op cit

13 Rimmer, L: op cit, p 44

14 Haskey, J: op cit

15 Leete, R and Anthony, S: 'Divorce and Remarriage: A record linkage study', *Population Trends 16,* OPCS/HMSO, 1979

16 Dunnell, K: op cit, p 39

David Clark

Marriage and Remarriage: New Wine in Old Bottles?

Despite the increasing availability of fairly detailed statistical and demographical data on the subject (ably summarised elsewhere in this volume) it appears that a striking feature of our theme of changing patterns of marriage and remarriage is how remarkably ignorant we remain about the *meaning* of it all. For whilst, with considerable confidence, we can give rates, frequencies and levels of divorce and remarriage, the underlying questions about why marriages break down and why divorced men and women go on to remarry remain largely unanswered. Still more daunting is the problem of understanding those deep-seated changes which may be taking place within the once familiar institution of the family—and the possible consequences which this may have for all aspects of social life in the future. Accordingly, my discusson here is couched in somewhat hesitant tones—born of the slipperiness of our subject matter. Moreover, I shall concentrate in the main upon the marital relationship, rather than upon parenthood, steprelations or whatever, in the belief that this provides a key with which to unlock numerous more deep-seated transformations in family life. In short I shall attempt to use 'marriage' in order to monitor a number of important changes which are currently taking place in the family.

Having said this it is appropriate to begin with the real world of experience by quoting two people who have taken part in a study which I have recently conducted in Aberdeen among a group of 25 newly married couples and 25 newly remarried couples.[1] Their comments, I believe, draw our attention to two of the central problems which we face in thinking about 'marriage' and 'remarriage'. The first of these is the often unacknowledged similarity in expectations of those who marry and those who remarry. The second is the emphasis, found in both cases, (marriage and remarriage) upon a notion of personal growth within the marriage relationship. It will become clear that these each have important implications for one another.

We begin with Mr Rowe,[2] aged 40, who has recently married for the second time.

> I don't think I expect the same sort of things from a relationship since my marriage failed . . . I think I've always felt that it was a bit ridiculous to expect

youngish people who had no experience of actually living with someone to get together in their twenties and still be together by the time they died. I don't think I'm going to change as much in the next 20, 30 years as I've changed in the last 15. So assuming (my new wife) doesn't change as much in the next 20, 30 years as in the last 15, I guess since we get on reasonably well now, there's a reasonable chance that we'll get on reasonably well in 20 years time. But I've certainly no longer got the feeling that because you marry someone, you'll automatically get on well with them for the rest of your life.

Mr Rowe's comments, perhaps surprisingly, find echoes in those of Mr Fenwick, who is 29 and has recently married for the first time.

If we grow together, then good. If we grow apart, then unfortunate. But it could happen. If we hang on . . . if the people that we change into are not too intolerable, then we'll simply carry on until we get back together again. If we drift too far apart, then that's just unfortunate. But there is a certain amount of determination on both sides to make it work and a great deal of awareness that this can happen.

The guarded optimism which these two statements have in common is probably at variance with some of our conventional assumptions about marriage and remarriage. In particular, I am thinking about the tendency to polarise the two into separate and discrete categories: the one essentially normal and taken-for-granted, the other (despite an increasing prevalence) still considered slightly deviant and the focus of special interest. I want to argue however that arbitrary comparisons between 'marriage' and 'remarriage' and any attempt to designate the two as separate institutions are of little worth. Remarriage can only exist if we have *marriage* and it is *marriage*—in its various forms—which should be the focus of attention.

Current figures suggest that the experience of divorce and remarriage will be encountered by an increasing proportion of the married population in the future. It is therefore possible that these transitions will be gradually incorporated into conventional expectations of the life cycle. Counselling ideologies and theories of personal growth may play a part in legitimating this process and could contribute to a greater sense of openess about 'successful' and 'unsuccessful' outcomes in marriage. Change in marriage is a worthy theme for a series of study days, yet it remains a daunting object for enquiry. Until it is more fully understood we are likely to remain poorly equipped to intervene in marital difficulties of any kind.

Privacy

One of the main reasons for this lack of understanding is the importance which we attach to the concept of *privacy* in marriage and family life. The nuclear family with its narrow policy and tawdry secrets may, as Leach[3] suggests, be the source of all our discontents, but for the time being—and despite a few broadsides from feminists and other radicals—we appear to want to keep it that way. The importance of privacy as a valued marital commodity cannot be over-stated. Marriage, or its surrogate, cohabitation, is of course a convenient means of establishing autonomy of living space—having 'a place of your own'. More importantly, the private sphere of home and family is itself then invested with complex meanings which ultimately are bound up with the quality of the marital relationship. 'Settling down', 'making a home', 'starting a family', thus signal particular turning points in the natural history of a marriage and are achieved in part through the successful creation and maintenance of a private world. Within this world, the couple are able to foster a sense of personal and joint identity,[4] which is often summed up in the popular term 'lifestyle'.

As a number of recent commentators have shown, this situation is conducive to a strong emphasis upon the *relational* aspects of marriage, and in particular the emotional, psychological and interpersonal rewards which marriage might deliver. Indeed, some have gone so far as to suggest that it is this very emphasis which leads to high rates of divorce (the by now familiar argument that divorce is symptomatic of taking marriage *more* rather than less seriously).

Marriage today, it has been suggested, is no longer to be lived vicariously— 'making the best of it'—but should be a source of fulfilment in and of itself. Not that fulfilment is always immediate, for marriage may be seen as a project, something as many couples in my study put it, 'to be worked at'. It therefore presents itself as a series of progressive goals and achievements—a continuous horizon of material, familial and emotional rewards which culminate in some elusive notion of a happy family life. Moreover, the conventional orthodoxies of counsellors and academics frequently underline this, emphasising marriage as a *process* rather than an institution.

As a result, the life course itself is progressively refined into new and neologistic phases. Childhood is sub-divided into a series of developmental stages; 'adolescence' appears (and then seems to get longer); 'early adulthood' ensues; the 'mid-life' becomes an autonomous stage (and is accordingly blessed with its own 'crisis'); finally, old age, once the privilege of the few, now takes increasing numbers beyond the traditonal three score and ten and brings in its wake a whole range of new duties and care obligations.

What do these life course refinements signify? Certainly a society concerned as never before with the *quality* of interpersonal relationships and therefore, we might argue, one in which the needs of the individual are given paramount importance—in other words a more humanitarian and caring society. Alternatively, we might suggest that this 'self' consciousness carries within it a kind of destructiveness. Richard Sennett's book *The Fall of Public Man* charts the history of this destructiveness through a process wherein 'We have tried to make the fact of being in private, alone with ourselves and with family and intimate friends, an end in itself.'[5] In other words, family life has become 'privatised', cut off from other aspects of life in a complex society. The family has thus become a place into which we *retreat* in order to 'relax' and 'be ourselves', but it is no longer, by and large, an institution having active inter-connections with the wider community. Indeed, faced with the increasing diversity of family living arrangements (the 'plurality of family forms') even willing policy-makers and administrators find themselves hard-pressed to consider 'the family' when debating issues of public relevance. The concerns of 'ordinary people in their families' therefore remain relatively invisible, and rarely reach the forefront of public scrutiny. Private life, in our attitudes, as in the law, remains both inviolable and hidden.

Divorce

Having said all this, there is one obvious phenomenon which brings the private world under the public microscope: mass divorce. In one sense it is not surprising that a society which has placed so much emphasis upon the pursuit of personal happiness should feel itself outraged by such a visible and momentous breakdown in personal relationships. Yet we might also feel it is this very emphasis which has produced the phenomenon in question. One thing is clear: divorce does not appear to diminish enthusiasm for marriage and for many, marital breakdown is rapidly followed by either cohabitation or remarriage. Yet despite its incidence, there appears to be only a small measure of comfort to be drawn from the knowledge that one is part of a 'trend' and for most people divorce is likely to be experienced more often than not as an isolated personal misery in the lives of a group of individuals hard-pressed to come to terms with it. For just as marriage requires meaning, so too does its break-up.

In particular, marital breakdown will require some rationalisation within the personal life cycle. Our beginning quotation represents one way in which this might be achieved through appeals to some implicit notion of personal growth and change. Such concepts, fashionably endorsed in therapeutic ideologies of various kinds, not only legitimate a broken relationship, but also allow a degree of confidence in the possible success of a future one— frequently in a trade-off between Dr Johnson's famous extremes of 'hope' and 'experience'. Yet even during the short span of my own research involvement in the study of divorce and remarriage there appear to have been subtle normative changes. In 1977 when Jackie Burgoyne and I first began contacting remarried couples for our Sheffield study,[6] it was common enough for them to remark with confidence that 'second marriages are likely to work better than first marriages'. Five years later in Aberdeen, such beliefs go unacknowledged and couples prefer instead to remain open to the probability of 'failure' and re-divorce. This caution is also evidenced by some newlyweds, aware of the implications of almost daily newspaper reports on 'British divorce mania'. Paradoxically, such a trend might be helpful if it serves to diminish the excesses of self-conscious 'constitution' and 'reconstitution' which may plague marriage and remarriage alike.

Public opinion however seems to retain high expectations of the marital relationship. In the summer of 1981 we conducted in Aberdeen and Sheffield a survey of public attitudes towards marriage, divorce and remarriage.[7] The survey showed unequivocally that the main reasons *why* people marry are inter-personal—to be with someone, share one's life with another, to care and be cared for were reasons cited by over 80 per cent of those interviewed. In both towns over 60 per cent of the sample felt that second marriages were less likely to end in divorce than first marriages and over 50 per cent thought that second marriages would be happier than the partners' first marriages (with under five per cent thinking they would be less happy). Certainly there is considerable pressure to succeed in a remarriage, for even if the public stigma attaching to divorce has now diminished, the sense of personal worth and esteem which is tied up in being 'happily married', remains enormous.

What then is 'being happily married'—either the first or the second time around? If people marry to share and be with another person and (less so, according to our survey) to have children, then a happy marriage should be one which fulfils these criteria. Yet clearly, other standards may be invoked. In talking in more detail to newlyweds and newly re-weds, it has proved difficult to tap in any systematic way the feelings which couples have about their marriages and the ways in which they might evaluate them. At one level the ingredients for a happy marriage consist of things like 'love', 'trust', 'honesty', 'having the same interests', all of which were commonly cited. But what do these add up to? 'Expectations of marriage', a term frequently used by professionals, often appear vague and weakly-formulated—in contrast to the clear-cut views with which couples are often accredited.

For example, I asked the newlyweds in my Aberdeen study 'what do you look forward to most in marriage?' One of the clearer replies came from 21-year-old Mrs Ferguson:

> I'm not very sure. It's not really having children anyway, I'm nae really looking forward to that, but then that grows on you I suppose. Uhm . . . I don't know . . . Our idea of marriage is being together and setting up a house together . . . and all the things you do when you're married that you don't do when you're single. But . . . er . . . what I'm really looking forward to . . . my aim in life . . . is to have a nice semi-detached or detached house . . . that's in the future. If my marriage just sallies on as it is, and gets on fine and we get everything organised, then I'll be happy.

Some of the men appeared even more vague. Mr Firth, aged 21:

> Just a long marriage . . . children . . . happy house . . . as I said before, I haven't really thought too much about that yet.

About a third of the newlyweds lived together before marriage and for some of these the experience of cohabitation appeared to have produced a more reflective approach to marriage. A 22-year-old woman who lived with her partner for three years before she was married made the following comments:

> Living together is just the same as marriage really, it's just a bit o' paper I always say. It's just that if you live together you can split up and that's it. If you get married you've divorces and a carry on. I would encourage people to do it. My cousin had a big wedding . . . she had a big limousine, big white wedding . . . and then, married for six months and then divorce. They had to sell a flat, everything, and then she said to me 'I wish I'd took your advice and bide in'. It just proves it that, I mean, all my family . . . well my sister, they lived together for three years and now they're happy, they've got a baby and everything now, they've got their own flat and everything. Most folks I ken that bide in first are happier than them that didnae ken each other before.

This is obviously linked in part to the notion of cohabitation as 'trial marriage'. Mr Fisher, aged 22:

> We were just living on our own—no worries or anything like that, so it was great. It taught me how to cook . . . it taught her how to cook for two . . . she didn't know how to cook. We learned a lot, she found out what I liked and what I disliked. I found out what she liked and what she didn't like. It was like an experiment.

The 'experiment' of cohabitation before making the commitment to marriage is however, despite its increasing popularity, less a feature of the build-up to *first* than to *second* marriage. Twenty one out of the 25 remarried couples interviewed were living together at the time of marriage. Most had decided to 'bide in' at first either through reluctance to commit themselves to a second marriage or because they were not yet free to marry. Several even appeared to have some fear that following a successful period of living together, formal remarriage could be a possible source of harm to their relationship. Mr Ryan, aged 38:

> The fact that you live with someone for an extended length of time makes you very aware that a lot of people are looking at you . . . watching you, and they're critical and they're saying, you know, 'I wonder how long that's going to last before it all breaks up', and subconsciously I'm sure you try a bloody sight harder to make it work than you might normally do if you were just straight married . . . so I think we worked a lot harder at living together than a lot of people do at being married and we've continued that in the married state. We still work quite hard at being together, trying not to be inconsiderate. It doesn't always work obviously, but I'm aware of working harder at it now than perhaps I ever did before. I think you take less for granted.

In general however, remarried couples did not seem to see remarriage as a watershed, nor were they able to contrast the earlier period of cohabitation with that of formal remarriage; for example, the decision to begin living together was often described as a more important one than the decision to remarry. In most cases both states 'felt the same'. Just occasionally, a couple might acknowledge some difference, but this seemed to be born as much of the belief that formal remarriage should be 'different', rather than any actual experience of change. Mr Rose, aged 46:

> I'm pleased with myself when I think that I'm married and I've married . . ., but I don't *feel* any different. I didn't feel . . . 'Oh, I should be different', 'oh, we should react towards each other differently'. That hasn't changed, we're still the same. But we sometimes think, well . . . we both think about it and . . . it's nice and we have a little smile to ourselves . . . it's nice, we like it.

Does remarriage produce any fundamental reappraisal of the institution of marriage? Do those who divorce and remarry engage in any basic critique of marriage, or are they looking only for greater compatability with their new partner than they had with the old? Most of the accounts which I have collected suggest the latter—embodied in a belief that it is not so much 'marriage' as the individual or couple which is at fault. Mrs Reynolds, aged 46, pursues the individualistic ethic.

> I still think it's up to the individual . . . however hard you work at it . . . 'cos you do have to work at any kind of partnership and marriage in particular. I really do think it's up to the individuals and some people don't work at it hard enough . . .

A common way of dealing with the question of altered expectations of marriage following divorce was through recourse once more to some notion of personal development—an appeal to changed personality or greater experience. Mr Rose uses a nice golfing analogy:

> It's like playing a game of golf. You've played the course three weeks previously and you can remember to go straight instead of going into the bog there, you play a little bit short so that you can play onto the green . . . you remember the mistake, or think you can. You think to yourself . . . 'oh! hold it now, I'm being a bit short-tempered here. I shouldn't do this, did I do it before?'

Perhaps the clinching remarks came from a divorced woman, who had remarried in her early thirties:

> Oh dear! What do you know at 22? What did I expect? I expected companion-ship and friendship and I found . . . disagreements and hostility. So what am I

looking for this time . . . .? More companionship and more friendship. It hasn't really changed my expectations . . . I didn't find it the first time, so I'm looking again.

I am suggesting therefore that despite some highly situated differences located in the experience of particular individuals, for most men and women the experience of divorce and remarriage is not accompanied by any major alterations in beliefs about marriage as an institution or a relationship. As Mrs Ryan, aged 36, put it:

I obviously think marriage is a good thing or I wouldn't have entered it again. But on the whole I think I have a fairly jaundiced view of actual marriages and seriously wonder if people are really getting very much out of it . . . that doesn't make me think that it's a bad thing in itself. I think it's a necessary thing.

Conclusions

We can usefully conclude by pondering on this a little further. Why should marriage be 'necessary'? So far, most of the ideas, expectations, beliefs and values relating to marriage which we have explored could potentially be realised within non-marital heterosexual or homosexual relationships of one sort or another. Those same interpersonal qualities which most of us cite as the main reasons for marriage are undoubtedly obtainable without matrimony. Why then, despite a recent shortfall, do most couples continue to seek formal, legal union?

Answers to this question finally compel us to look beyond the private to the public sphere. Despite the atrophy of family functions within society and the well-documented shift which the family has undergone from a unit of production to a unit of consumption, there remain certain crucial areas of contact between families and the wider society. One of these, as we have seen, is at the normative level. The 'retreat' into personal relationships and the private sphere does not take place in a vacuum. Powerful norms—especially those communicated through mass communications media and advertising present us with models of idealised family life. In countless subtle and not-so-subtle ways we are continually reminded of the 'appropriateness' of marriage within our culture.

Marriage also has numerous expedient and pragmatic advantages in terms of accommodation, income, standard of living and so on. Feminists have, of course, argued that most of these advantages pertain to men, rather than women, since typically it is women who sacrifice career and earning power in order to become unpaid workers in the home. Taking that perspective it is possible to arrive at a number of more trenchant answers to the question—'why marry?'—since marriage could be seen as an institution essentially concerned, within a male-dominated society, with the perpetration of inequalities between men and women. Current post-divorce arrangements, for example, provide an interesting guide to more deeply-based assumptions. For example, debates about financial settlement at divorce and continuing financial support highlight the issue of financial dependence within marriage. Arguments about whether divorced men should continue to financially support their ex-wives cannot be separated from the wider problem of how financial obligations are distributed within the home. Continuing financial support *appears* to be contrary to the principle of women's liberation, yet to abolish it may adversely affect the interests of ex-wives who may have lived through sometimes lengthy marriages characterised by male financial dominance—women who, generally speaking, will have had poor experiences in the labour and educational markets.

In the case of disputes over custody, we see the knife cutting the opposite way. Eighty-five to 90 per cent of custody cases result in custody going to the mother. To what extent does this merely reinforce the *de facto* situation wherein women, even within on-going marriages, are largely responsible for care and control of the children? 'Equality' should, of course, allow equitable custody opportunities to both parents, yet in practice the 'natural' principle—or rather the one deeply-entrenched in our system of family organisation—tends to prevail.

It is perhaps in the context of childbearing and parenthood that some of these difficulties find their most graphic expression. The desire to have children may, as our survey has suggested,[8] come a poor second to adult personality needs when deciding *whether* to marry, but the prospect of children is still a powerful motivation for marriage. Ninety per cent of all children in Britain are born into legal marriages. Moreover, the desirability of this seems to be shared by those in first and second marriages alike. One third of the remarried couples in my present study had finally decided to marry when faced with the arrival of their own child. Indeed, something like one fifth of all children are now born into remarriages of one sort or another. For most of these their parents' remarriage and the presence of step- and non-custodial siblings will be a 'normal' and 'taken-for-granted' part of family life.

Marriage and remarriage on a mass scale may be harbingers of dramatic and deep changes in family life. Yet so far it seems that the very *incidence* of divorce and remarriage has run ahead of our ability to cope with it. Certainly the current retreat into the private sphere and an over investment in the domestic world— what Sennett calls 'the tyrannies of intimacy'[9]—seem doomed to failure, being themselves agents of further marital unhappiness. We face two sets of difficulties. The first, which I have emphasised most here though it may not be the most important, concerns our understanding of inter-personal relationships within marriage. The second concerns the organisation of marital *roles* and *obligations* and their relationship to broader legal, economic and normative structures. Without a fundamental reappraisal of both we may be condemned to recommitting the errors of the past. For the moment however, it seems that *r*emarriage is not the solution to contradictions which are endemic to marriage.

References and notes

1 All of the couples were married in Aberdeen in 1981; they make up a self-selected, non-random group who took part in the study after replying to a letter outlining the project, which they received in the post along with their marriage licence. I should like to thank the Registrar General for Scotland and his Aberdeen staff for their co-operation in the study

2 All names used here are pseudonyms taken from the Aberdeen telephone directory. Names beginning with 'r' denote remarried couples, those beginning with 'f' are first marriages

3 Leach, E R: *A Runaway World,* London: BBC, 1968

4 Berger, P L and Kellner, H: 'Marriage and the Construction of Reality', *Diogenes,* pp 1-23, 1964

5 Sennett, R: *The Fall of Public Man,* Cambridge University Press, 1977, p 4

6 Burgoyne, J and Clark, D: 'Why Get Married Again?', *New Society,* 52, (913), 3 April 1980
'Parenting in Stepfamilies' in Chester, R and Diggory, P (eds): *Changing Patterns of Child-bearing and Child Rearing,* London, Academic Press, 1981
'Starting Again? Problems and Expectations in Remarriage', *Marriage Guidance,* September 1981
'From Father to Stepfather' in McKee, L and O'Brien, M (eds): *The Father Figure,* London, Tavistock, 1982

7 The 'Family Beliefs Survey' was conducted by the author and Jackie Burgoyne, with the assistance of SCPR, in both Aberdeen and Sheffield in 1981. A full report of the study is in preparation and further details can be obtained from the author

8 The FBS showed that 'having children' was mentioned as a reason for marriage on 37 per cent of possible occasions in Sheffield and 31 per cent in Aberdeen

9 Sennett, R: *op cit,* conclusion

Discussion

In many ways, the discussion during the day was trying to find common ground between pairs which might appear as opposites or incompatible.

Marriage as a private and yet public issue. One marriage or divorce is the concern of the individuals involved, but the sum statistics for marriage or divorce have become a public issue.

Marriage as a community concern or a government concern. Lesley Rimmer stressed the importance of a family perspective in public policy, and showed how such policy limits the ways people may choose to live their lives.

Marriage and its problems as the province of practitioners or experts in the research field. Nicholas Tyndall talked about the difficulties experienced by practitioners in making constructive use of the data presented by researchers. It is important to develop a research attitude to practice, maybe through the simple monitoring of cases or clients.

Marriage and remarriage as fundamentally the same or different. The experience of divorce is a traumatic one for everybody involved, wider family and friends as well as the couple and their children. Lesley Rimmer, in support of her contention that divorce should not be an adversarial process, cited the fact that the non-custodial parent, who in over 80 per cent of cases is the father, often loses touch with his children in a very short time. The point was also made that not only parenting, but also grandparenting is lost in divorce.

Thus the undeniable difference between first marriage and remarriage is that one or both partners have been through divorce, and when children are involved, marriage takes on an extra dimension—step parenting.

The discussion also touched on the issues of cohabitation, working wives, unemployment, and expectations of marriage. Is cohabitation an effective prelude to marriage? The statistics suggest that it is not, as divorced people are more likely to have lived with their partners before marriage than others. The break up of long term cohabiting relationships may not be as simple as people think, and such breakups, seen quite often in probation work, are masked in the divorce statistics.

The possible connections between marriage breakdown and unemployment, and marriage breakdown and working wives, were explored. There is more unemployment amongst divorced and separated men than amongst married men, but there is no evidence to suggest that one causes the other—that unemployment increases the risk of marriage breakdown, or that marriage breakdown increases the risk of unemployment.

As far as the second suggestion is concerned—that women going out to work may be a contributory factor in causing marriage breakdown—both speakers were strong in their denial that there is any such simple pattern, even though going out to work and meeting a wider circle of people may cause women to question what was already a bad relationship. But the question about wives as workers raised the challenge—what about men as fathers? Fathers of young children working regular overtime cannot fully undertake their responsibilities as fathers and this puts further pressure on their wives.

However, marriage has to be looked at in the social context of the time in which the couple got married. This means that marriages of three and of 20 years are not just different in length, but also in the expectations the couples had about issues like these—work and parental responsibility.

In talking about expectations of marriage, and in particular the inarticulated expectations young people may have, the question was asked 'is it possible to bridge the gap between expectations, as perpetuated in our social norms, and reality?'. Lesley Rimmer, although in sympathy with the idea that education should be a prerogative, doubted if old heads could be put on young shoulders. David Clark pointed out that organisations such as the Marriage Guidance Council may be contributing to the problems they try to deal with by raising people's expectations of personal fulfilment.

London, 8 July 1982:

Changing Roles of Men and Women and the Effects on the Family

Chairman   *Sir Patrick Nairne,* Master, St Catherine's College, Oxford. Formerly Permanent Secretary, Department of Health and Social Security.

Speakers   *Martin Richards, MA, PhD,* Child Care and Development Group, University of Cambridge. Research into parent-child relationships and aspects of developmental psychology. Books include *Race, Culture and Intelligence* (Editor with K Richardson, J Spears) Penguin Books, 1972. *Fathers and Fatherhood* (under contract) Penguin Books.

Pauline Crabbe, OBE, JP, Vice-Chairman, Brook Advisory Centres. Formerly involved with the National Council for the Unmarried Mother and her Child, and with a longstanding interest in race relations.

Gill Gorell Barnes, Family Therapy Programme, Department for Children and Parents, Tavistock Clinic. Senior Social Worker and family therapist.

Introduction

This day might have been seen as 'preaching to the converted' as nobody disputed that changes are taking place in men and women's roles in marriage. But an acceptance of change does not necessarily include an understanding of the implications of that change, and it was these implications that the speakers and participants were struggling to understand.

Pauline Crabbe said challenges to established patterns of behaviour such as those embodied in the traditional institution of marriage should be regarded as healthy and not seen as threats. As a women's magazine problem page editor said, organisations like the National Marriage Guidance Council should be more ready to point out the positive aspects of change to balance the somewhat gloomy picture which prevails of a worthy institution falling apart.

Martin Richards started off with a paper on the roles of men as husbands and fathers, followed by Pauline Crabbe talking about women and marriage today. The third speaker was Gill Gorell Barnes, who talked about children in changing circumstances, drawing on her experience as a family therapist.

Martin Richards
The Changing Role of Men

There can be few social institutions which are as widely and continually discussed as the family. There is a general belief that the family is changing and a substantial number of people appear to believe that all changes are for the worse. Indeed, there is a constant tendency to compare the family of today with a supposedly superior one that was thought to exist at some point in the past. As the historians of the family have begun to teach us, few of the features that are thought to be characteristic of the families of the past have much foundation in fact. The multigenerational extended family, for instance, seems to have been very rare in pre-industrial England. The late age at marriage and shorter life span meant it was unlikely that many children had surviving grandparents.[1]

The fact that the family is seen to be such a central institution in our society and that we are all so emotionally engaged in it is the probable explanation for all the myths that seem to exist about it and they also make detached analysis of family life a difficult enterprise. In this paper I want to examine some aspects of lives of men in contemporary English families, particularly with respect to their roles as fathers and husbands. In each case I want to suggest that important changes are taking place but that these are more complex, and in certain respects contradictory, than is generally believed. My message is not a gloomy one, at least for those who may have feared that family life is seriously threatened, for it is my belief that, as so often in the past, the family is adapting to changing circumstances and is at no risk of disappearing. However, the forms in which it may persist are ones that will not necessarily appeal to the more conservative members of our society.

Men as fathers

It is widely believed that the contemporary father is more involved with his children than has been the case in the recent past. The evidence for such claims comes from a variety of sources—from advice books for parents for instance. It is not only that the most recent editions of long running classics like Dr Spock

121

have rapidly expanded their discussion of fathers but a whole new range of books aimed at the male parent have appeared in recent years.* Of course, we might object that advice books are not necessarily a reflection of what people are doing. Indeed, but the authors and publishers of paperbacks do have a good idea of what people want to read. So even if these books do not reflect an increasing concern of fathers with their children they do show that parents are interested in reading about the role of the father. The same comment could be made about the recent royal birth. From the time that the pregnancy was first announced a great deal of the press comment concerned the father and his involvement in the pregnancy. A superficial look at some back files suggests that such comment was more or less absent in previous royal births.

A second source of evidence is that provided by social historians. A little reading in this area begins to indicate how complex matters are and that many simple statements about increases or decreases in fathers' involvement are likely to be gross simplifications. What fathers did was widely variable between communities and across time. We also encounter more myths about the past. Interestingly these are not all of the golden days that have been sadly lost, but in the matter of fatherhood are also of bad old days now thankfully past.

Young and Willmott[2] writing of the working class man pre second world war state, 'The husband was not only mean with money. He was callous in sex, as often as not forcing a trial of unwanted pregnancies upon his unwilling mate. He was harsh to his children. He was violent when drunk, which was often'.

Lummis,[3] who quotes this passage, carried out an interview study among old people (average date of birth 1893) in an East Anglian fishing community and came to the very different conclusion that 'working-class marriage was in fact more generally an affectionate partnership of caring parents jointly concerned with preserving the family'. While there are obvious problems about the accuracy of long remembered facts, the rate of use of physical punishment, for instance, reported by Lummis are lower than many contemporary studies.

The third source of data are studies of contemporary fathers. Here we are increasingly well served by a very active group of researchers who have created a major area of growth in developmental psychology. Already there are two substantial books reporting their findings.[4, 5] Many of their studies do suggest that fathers are doing more with their children[6] but like the historians' work indicate that the whole matter is far from simple. It is not just that the degree of father participation varies with such factors as the age and sex of the children (generally, higher participation with older children and boys) but that the whole idea of 'participation' itself is to some extent misleading.[7]

---

*Some current examples from the United States which seems to be the world leader in the field:

   Father Feelings (Daley, 1977). 'A heartlifting book for every dad, every child and every mother who loves them both!'

   Father Power (Biller and Meredith, 1975). 'The art of effective fathering and how it can bring joy and freedom to the whole family.'

   How to Father (Dobson, 1974). 'A miracle . . . a must for every father—move over, Dr Spock!'

Many studies have tried to measure participation by using lists of activities that a father might or might not do. These indicate that while most fathers play with their children, only a small minority change nappies or feed small infants.[8] Overall ratings of participation are usually derived by combining the various activities so that the most participant fathers do the most activities most frequently. However, what studies adopting this kind of orientation miss is that the division of labour in the home is a matter to be negotiated and that couples reach a very wide variety of arrangements. As McKee[9] argues it is quite possible for a father to be very involved with his children and very participant without doing any of the things on the conventional checklists of child care activities (or the reverse). Participation is a much more subtle concept. Another weakness of the 'participation' studies is that the mother is often used as the source of information about what the father does. Despite these difficulties these studies make clear that while most men do some caretaking for their children, compared with their partners, their rates are low.

In general, outside social class I and II families, mothers' expectations about their partner's child care activities were also low. Our experience,[10] like others, is of mothers who would report a minimal level of caretaking from husbands who they would describe as 'marvellous' or 'one in a million'.

What does seem to be characteristic of middle class families, and to a lesser extent elsewhere, is a high level of conflict for men between work and home life.[11] Both partners in these families often expressed an ideal of more or less equal participation in child care but saw the fathers' role severely but necessarily limited by their work commitments. O'Brien comments that when questioned many middle class men spoke with regret and guilt about their limited parental roles. On the other hand working class fathers expressed much less work-home conflict and perceived their work as being for their families. As O'Brien sums it up: 'The middle-class fathers' stated qualitarian attitudes concerning family responsibilities were not, in this study at least, necessarily demonstrated in practical ways. This disjunction between attitude and behaviour was also true for the working class men, but here the pattern was directly reversed, working class men were actually involved more than they felt proper.'

Fathers at birth

An area in which change has been clear and unambiguous is in the presence of fathers at the birth of their children. Over the last two or three decades there has been a complete shift so that something that was rare (except perhaps at home births) has now become commonplace and expected. Expected, for instance, in the recent royal birth. There are probably a whole variety of reasons for this sudden change.[12] These range from women's needs for companionship in the isolated and impersonal atmosphere which is found in too many maternity hospitals to an emphasis on pregnancy and birth as a shared family process.

The involvement of fathers in their partner's pregnancy and delivery has been much studied by the new generation of father researchers.[13, 14, 15, 16, 17, 18, 19, 20] While fathers often seem delighted and overwhelmed by the experience of seeing their children born and there are suggestions that this may reinforce their

123

relationship with their child,[21, 22] there are some features of the situation that should cause us to hesitate before accepting the new norm too readily. We should note that presence of fathers at birth is culturally very rare as well as being a very recent development in our own society. While this in itself is no argument against (think of infant mortality, for instance), it should cause us to enquire more closely into the reasons and the consequences. One point is that it may reflect a declining solidarity among women over matters related to reproduction and the growing power and domination of male professionals. Non-professional information is often denigrated as being 'old wives' tales' yet professional practice may have no firmer basis. Mother-daughter and mother-mother links may have been weakened by the social isolation of the nuclear family. It is significant that much of the energy of the women's movement has been concerned with spreading knowledge and support over matters related to reproduction.

For men, too, their presence at birth may create conflicts and uncertainties. Not only is their role in the delivery room unclear and uncertain but it may also emphasise to them the extent to which experiences cannot be shared with their partner and that the whole ideology of shared parenthood is too simplistic. For first time fathers this realisation may cause a sudden and deep disappointment which can place a great strain on the couple's relationship. While the connections between the arrival of children and the breakdown of marriages is complex,[23] there is little doubt that the birth of a child is often the start of the process of decay.

Marriage and divorce

Perhaps the most widely recognised trend in family life has been the rise in the divorce rate. In England and Wales the number of petitions filed for dissolutions and annulments of marriage rose from about 30,000 in 1960 to about 170,000 in 1980. Looking at this in another way, more than a quarter of marriages are likely to end in divorce.[24] But these figures do not seem to reflect any headlong flight from marriage as the tendency to remarry after divorce has kept step with the divorce figures, at least until very recently. One in three of all marriages involve at least one partner who has married at least once before. Taking a wider time perspective we might note that probably a larger proportion of the population marries at least once than has been the case since records began over a century ago. Certainly, the proportion who marry more than once is at an all time high. In this sense marriage has never been more popular.

It has been suggested that current divorce rates reflect more a change in women's roles than men's and, in particular, relate to an increased economic independence for some women. Engels may have rather over-simplified matters when he said that the first premise for the emancipation of women is the reintroduction of the entire female sex into public industry[25] but he at least clearly recognised the implication of employment patterns and economic independence for family life. But, of course, not all the significant changes have been economic and there have been considerable shifts in aspirations and values about relationships and, not least, in patterns of sexual behaviour which have all played a part in the rise of divorce.

The majority of divorce petitions are brought by women. It would be naive to assume that this necessarily reflects a greater female dissatisfaction with marriage. The legal process of divorce, in practice, is about dividing property, and settling maintenance and arrangements for children. These are matters which are of particular concern to women who are most likely to remain primarily responsible for the children and are least likely to be the major wage earner.

At divorce women retain custody in about 80 per cent of cases and the evidence suggests that within a few years of a separation only about a half of all fathers are in regular contact with their children.[26] The basic reason for this pattern is that the same assumptions that exist about the care of children during marriage persist through divorce.[27] Unfortunately, it is also the case that the same factors that tend to promote the welfare of children within a marriage also persist beyond divorce and these include an effective relationship with both parents.[28] There is little doubt that our current pattern of marriage, remarriage and divorce serves the interests of adults much better than children[29] and much more could and should be done to protect the interests of children.[30]

The pattern of fatherhood portrayed by the divorce research stands in complete contrast to that seen in 'intact' families. Present patterns mean that a significant minority of fathers are living separately from their children and many of these have lost all contact with them. But like everything in family life even this picture has another side because it is clear that for some men a divorce is the beginning of a close relationship with their children. There are not just the small groups who become custodial parents[31, 32] but also those who do make satisfactory access arrangements and find that having sole responsibility for child care for part of the time may lead to a new and more satisfying parental relationship.

The other obvious implication of current trends is the growing diversity of family forms. Single parent families will be the lot of many for at least some of their lives but, in addition, there are a whole range of what Americans call 'blended' families in which there are step relationships of various kinds. In addition, there are new kinds of visiting parent-child relations set up in the wake of divorce. In the midst of the pain and confusion which surrounds divorce there is the evolution of new patterns of family life some of which may provide good models for more satisfying family life for both parents and children.

Some other trends

There are many other trends in society which are either the product of or have considerable implications for the relationships of men and women. Among the most important are likely to be the falling birth rate, the growing proportion of old people in the population, the relative increase in employment among mothers and the rising rates of overall unemployment. There is not space to give any of these topics the space they deserve but I think it would be wrong to end without saying a little about one of them, unemployment. The family may have, for some, become a haven from work but this does not mean that it is not profoundly influenced by economic and political changes outside. An obvious and dramatic example of this is unemployment. I think we are too easily led to assume that the present economic situation is temporary and when it passes employment patterns will revert to those of a decade or so ago. Productivity and the new technologies mean fewer jobs and unless we make radical changes in the nature of employment we are going to have a considerable number of adults without paid work in the foreseeable future. In a society where most men have and expect to have paid work outside the home, unemployment can have a negative and disastrous effect on family life. But, of course, it is not simply that the family is influenced by outside economic and social factors but also that influence passes in the other direction. It is my guess that repercussion for families of the present economic situation may generate the factors that leads to change and what is going on in some families may have far reaching economic and political effects.

References

1 Laslett, P: *The World We Have Lost,* Methuen, 2nd edn, 1971

2 Young, M and Willmott, P: *Family and Kinship in East London,* Penguin, 1962

3 Lummis, T: 'The Historical Dimension of Fatherhood: A case study 1890-1914' in McKee, L and O'Brien, M (eds): *The Father Figure,* Tavistock, 1982

4 McKee, L and O'Brien, M (eds): *The Father Figure,* Tavistock, 1982

5 Beail, N and McGuire, J: *Psychological Aspects of Fatherhood,* London: Junction Books, 1982

6 Lewis, C, Newson, E and Newson, J: 'Father Participation through Childhood and its Relationship with Career Aspirations and Delinquency' in Beail and McGuire, op cit

7 McKee, L: 'Father's Participation in Infant Care: A critique' in McKee and O'Brien, op cit

8 Richards, MPM, Dunn, J F and Antonis, B: 'Caretaking in the First Year of Life', *Child Care, Health and Development,* 3, 23-36, 1977

9 McKee, L: op cit

10 Richards, Dunn and Antonis: op cit

11 O'Brien, M: 'The Working Father' in Beail and McGuire, op cit

12 Richards, MPM: 'Husbands Becoming Fathers'. Paper presented at a seminar on the impact of children on marriage, April 1980.

13 Scott-Heyes, G: 'The Experience of Perinatal Paternity and its Relation to Attitudes to Pregnancy and Childbirth' in Beail and McGuire, op cit

14 Brown, A: 'Fathers in the Labour Ward: Medical and lay accents' in McKee and O'Brien, op cit

15 Lewis, C: 'A Feeling You Can't Scratch?: The effect of pregnancy and birth on married men' in Beail and McGuire, op cit

16 Richards, MPM (1980): op cit

17 Woollet, A, White, D and Lyon, L: 'Observations of Fathers at Birth' in Beail and McGuire, op cit

18 Richman, J: 'Men's Experiences of Pregnancy and Chilbirth' in McKee and O'Brien, op cit

19 Beail, N: 'The Role of the Father During Pregnancy and Childbirth' in Beail and McGuire, op cit

20 Richmond, J and Goldthorp, WO: 'Fatherhood: The social construction of pregnancy and birth' in Kitzinger, S and Davis, JA (eds): *The Place of Birth,* Oxford University Press, 1978

21 Greenberg, M and Morris N: 'Engrossment: The newborn's impact upon the father', *American Journal of Orthopsychiatry,* 44, 520-531, 1974

22 Rodholm, M: 'Effects of Father-Infant Postpartum Contact on the Interactions Three Months After Birth', *Early Human Development,* 5, 79-85, 1981

23 Richards, MPM and Dyson, M: *Separation, Divorce and the Development of Children: A review,* unpublished report for the DHSS, 1982

24 Leete, R: 'Marriage and Divorce', *Population Trends,* 3, 3-8, HMSO, 1976

25 Engels, F: *The Origins of the Family, Private Property and the State,* 1884. 1972 edition published by Lawrence and Wishart.

26 Eekelaar, J and Clive, E: *Custody After Divorce,* Family Law Studies No 1, Oxford: Centre for Socio-Legal Studies, 1977

27 Richards, MPM: 'Post-Divorce Arrangements for Children: A Psychological Perspective', *J Social Welfare Law,* 133, 151, 1982

28 Richards, MPM and Dyson, M: op cit

29 Burgoyne, J and Clark, D: 'From Father to Step-Father' in McKee and O'Brien, op cit

30 Richards, MPM (1982): op cit

31 Hipgrave, T: 'Lone Fatherhood: A problematic status' in McKee and O'Brien, op cit

32 O'Brien, M: 'Becoming a Lone Father: Differential patterns and experiences' in McKee and O'Brien, op cit

Pauline Crabbe

The Changing Role of Women

The key to my thoughts lies in the March issue of *Marriage Guidance,* where it says: 'The therapist has to recognise that change is seen as a threat. It will be resisted tenaciously—at times as though it were a threat to survival.' It occurred to me that I feel that way very strongly about change, and when I was asked to take part in the study day I realised that I wanted in fact to resist the whole idea of coming here and sharing my observations with you. I wanted to block out the whole thing, and when I was asked about the various important changes that have taken place, I wanted to get rid of them by saying—the ruling class no longer rule; the working class no longer work; and the middle class are no longer in the middle. But as a survivor of change, both in my personal and my professional life, I thought I would go a little more deeply into it than that and tell you how I feel the recent changes in our society have affected the role of women in marriage.

I propose to do this by first of all highlighting the social backdrop against which we react to the changes, then by drawing an identikit picture of three groups of women. I will finish by giving you my own personal short checklist which has helped me to cope with changes. So let's start by having a look at the social fabric—the backdrop against which we play out our roles in marriage.

At the moment we are in the aftermath of the sexual revolution. No longer is marriage the price that men have to pay for sex, or sex the price that women have to pay for marriage. But side by side with that there has been a massive breakdown in personal relationships which can be summed up by looking at three figures. One child in every nine stands the chance of being without one natural parent before he reaches the age of 11. One person in every six will spend time in their lives having some form of psychiatric care, and that is often —not always but often—the result of a breakdown in personal relationships. In inner cities until two years ago the fourth commonest cause of death was suicide, which again indicates a breakdown in personal relationships. That figure has changed and lessened but unfortunately there is now an increase in what I call the self mutilation diseases, alcohol abuse, drug abuse, anorexia and so on.

That's the background against which we look at technological and social changes, and I am going to single out the ones that I see as especially significant in the lives of women. I have divided them into advances made in physical machinery, and advances made in medical, legal, and social machinery.

Physically, we've seen the tremendous advances in housing and lift design which have resulted in high rise flats and denied us gardens and easy access across the garden fence. High rise flats in the inner cities have influenced our children's education—not education for jobs, but education for living.

We have had the development of household aids which have given women increased leisure but not at the same time given us an alternative sense of purpose. Household drudgery gave a sense of purpose to many women.

We have the innovation of the supermarket, where the mass of convenience foods have to be paid for in cash and increase the opportunities for shop lifting. The advance of the supermarket and payment in cash has been a terrible disadvantage to poor women because the corner shop has disappeared, where if you ran out of money on a Monday or Tuesday you could have it chalked up on the slate until the end of the week.

Improvements in industrial machinery have militated against the vast army of the unskilled labour force amongst which women are very strongly represented.

The increased mobility of whole families is another change. When we are faced with mobility, women are then faced with extra pressures. Even if the woman has a good job, in which she is making a contribution to the breadwinning activities and which is helping her personally to achieve her own potential, it is almost always the woman who has to give up her job to move. It is only very recently with a small number of young people where discussion goes on between the husband and wife as to which of them should give up their job and move.

Alongside this, changes have taken place with regard to the movement away from home which young people need to undertake as part of their development. There are a great many approved ways of moving away from home as far as the middle classes are concerned because they can always go to University if they've got their As, or go into training as nurses, or go to college, or share a flat with friends. All these are approved ways of getting away from home. The poorer sections of the community don't have these choices. They are always the ones whose choices are much more limited and very often the only way they can get away from home is by getting married or getting pregnant.

We have the improved machinery of divorce, with its spin off of one in three marriages being remarriages. There we are faced with a tremendous change in the role of women in the family because many women have had to take on the role of step-parent. This means learning a new aspect of parenting as step parenting is quite different from natural parenting.

We have more aids to help us to control our fertility, and today we have the first generation who are able to challenge the euphemistic words 'family planning', and make their demands known for safe sex.

Those are an outline of some of the changes and how they affect us. Now let me paint the identikit picture of the three groups with whom I am familiar.

The first group is a group about whom we are rather ashamed and so we use a lot of euphemisms to describe them. We talk about the disadvantaged, the under privileged, classes five and six, and even the 'financially disabled'. What we really mean are poor people—people who suffer from the disease of poverty and its secondary infection, apathy.

It is not just material poverty but poverty of opportunity. Women who are known as women with multi-problems find it much harder to take advantage of change. For instance these women find it very difficult to make the most of improved methods of birth control for very simple reasons. If you are the mother of a large family, and you've got one child in and out of care, and a partner who is in and out of the betting shop, or the pub, and certainly in and out of work, and if the electricity is going to be cut off tomorrow, birth control is a fairly low priority.

Then we have another group and this group is one again described by a great many euphemisms, perhaps for the same reason that we are rather ashamed of them. In 1962, or the early 60s, a new collective noun crept into the English language. Well, this new collective noun was an 'embarrassment of immigrants', because we had those euphemistically described as coming from different ethnic minorities or coloured people, where in fact we really meant blacks. For this section of our multi-racial society the changes of roles in marriage for women have been as traumatic in a different way. They have had to cope with cultural pressures, and conflicts which have arisen within the family.

For the Asian community, a patriarchal society for whom marriage has tremendous importance, changes are hard to accept. Female children are taught that their aim in life is to be chosen in marriage—not because they are beautiful or because they will get a good dowry but because they are likely to be able to look after the elderly people when they can no longer look after themselves. Arranged marriages, which are still part of the background, culture and religion of many members of the Asian community, may cause difficulties within families where young women were born and bred in this country. These young women find a conflict for them wanting to choose their own mate and the old ideas that they should submit to the choice in an arranged marriage.

With regard to the West Indians, the picture is slightly different because we are a matriarchal society. Marriage has never been quite our scene. We have, after all, been influenced by the slave heritage in which we were not allowed to marry. We were encouraged to have children, because every child added to the riches of the master's estate, but were not allowed to marry, and men were not allowed to have any legal responsibility towards their children. So women had to take on all the responsibilities in their own homes. West Indians put a high intrinsic value on children, and we pay tribute to the life force, which makes it again difficult to take advantage of aids in birth control. We have conflicts within our family because we have strict standards of behaviour for our children, but we find that caring for other people's children is not difficult for us because we have always included other people's children as part of our family.

Now I come to the third group and we have no euphemisms to describe these and so I simply call them 'the guilty'. They are represented in all the other groups I have mentioned and they are that mass of women who bear a burden of guilt thrust upon us by a society rich in double standard thinking.

We are made to feel guilty if we have large families; we are made to feel guilty if we don't have any children at all; we are made to feel guilty if we are not all sexual athletes and having multiple orgasms night after night; we are made to feel very guilty if when we are divorced we leave children with our partners and don't fight for their custody; the young ones are made to feel guilty if they don't get married; older women are made to feel guilty if they can't cope with their teenage children and can't continue with the burden of caring for their elderly parents; we are often made to feel guilty in remarriage when we take on other people's children and find it too difficult to learn the new craft of step-parenting. One of the most difficult areas in step-parenting is learning how to use the language of touch which is very important, particularly with adolescent boys to help them remove the taboo on tenderness with which their peer group surrounds them.

Young people are now challenging the institution of marriage. They are the ones that are trying to get us to move away from the nuclear family and make it perhaps the unclear family. They have different attitudes to families and we should listen to them. If they don't want to get married, they may be holding out for living together—perhaps for a period, perhaps for life—but there is a great deal of guilt imposed upon them regardless of their reasons.

So that's a picture of some groups of women and the changes that affect them. I have inferred how they have or have not coped with changes. One of the bad things I think we have done is to use up a lot of our energy in coping with the changes, rather than using it to improve and strengthen the relationships between us and our partners. And so, to end, I'm going to give you one or two points on a checklist which I have found quite useful.

I think that we have to regain our resilience if we are going to continue to cope with change, and we can do that by conserving our social and emotional energy and not wasting it in regretting the past—the past is done. Let's look at the positive achievements. The growth, for instance, of the sharing community which now shares the role of the family, and the responsibility of caring for the family. Women have played a very, very important role in nurturing that. We have to learn new skills, amongst them the skill of step-parenting, and let us continue to draw on the mutual support that we get from other women, but accept with appreciation and warmth the encouragement given to us by men who must with us face the menacing threat of change.

Gill Gorell Barnes

Children in Changing Circumstances

How do we conceptualise a family?

Families are constructed of individual people interacting together over time. These interactions become patterned in particular ways around family tasks and areas of shared activity, and the feelings and emotions that become associated with these which affect the development of future patterns and the possibilities that are open to the family. Looking at a family, we can ask as outsiders, how is this pattern organised over time around the areas of activity that are required for the successful development of children? What are the particular features of the way 'this family' has organised, and do these ways form a matrix or cluster of aspects of necessary parenting that are good enough for the child—for the child's psychological, emotional, affectional, social and cognitive development, given the age and stage he's at.

So that when we are thinking about a family we try and look at the way the pattern is organised over time, the life cycle development of the child in the family, the age and stage he's at, and how this particular family copes with the required adaptations that are posed by each age and stage. All healthy families have to go through pretty radical adaptation. Babies interrupt the two person process of early marriage and they may sever or intensify the parents' relationship with their own parents. Toddlers create a shock by saying 'no' for the first, second and three hundredth time, and some mothers can't stand it—the incidence of battering goes up at around this age. Children go to school, and mothers find that difficult too (school phobia develops). Children become teenagers, dye their hair green, stick safety pins in their ears. While nobody enjoys this in the older generation it does require appropriate adaptation for the family as a whole, and from parents in particular, not to become a major issue with inappropriately disruptive effect.

What sort of 'ideal' family do we hold in our minds?

We may all wish for children to have stable, loving families which provide emotional support, social stability, and cognitive stimulation. Luckily most families do provide what Donald Winnicott called 'good enough' parenting. This concept remains peculiarly difficult to define. What are the qualities that children require in order to develop without the development of psychiatric symptoms? How can we identify the sources of social competence and the development of coping skills and identify the nature of protective influences that are offered by different family structures whether these are two parent, one parent or multi parent? The gist of my contribution then is to look not at what has changed for children, because this would be difficult to identify. Family mobility, working mothers, loss of parents by illness or accident, various kinds of family disruption have characterised family life for many centuries. The loss of parents by divorce is a relatively new phenomenon but we should not assume it is necessarily harmful in the long term. Children are adaptive organisms with peculiar and individual forms of resilience. But in the face of change we also need to remember what constraints should be preserved, and to know about the minimum nurturing environment in which children can develop, and how this is different at different ages and stages, as a base line to thinking about the forms in which these ideas can be maintained in spite of changes in family style and structure.

A very short short list is culled from some of the research summarised by Michael Rutter in *Helping Troubled Children*.[1] He has identified the absence or gross distortion of parenting in the following areas as correlating with psychiatric disorder in children. The nature of the affectional bonds, whether the child has a secure base from which to explore; the quality of parental models for conscious and unconscious imitation; the quality of interaction between parents, verbal, emotional and sexual; whether the child has developed mentally appropriate life experience, and by this we mean things as simple as food, warmth, social stimulation, play; the quality of discipline; and the communication network both inside the family and between the family and the outside world. The presence of grossly distorted styles of dealing with stress like drinking, violence and perpetual recourse to illness or drug abuse, can also lead to disorder in the children.

I am going to go back to attachment as a key construct. It's a construct orginally developed in this country by Dr John Bowlby and it remains central to the successful development of children, acting as a bridge between the child's internal instinctual needs and the family behaviours which develop in response to these. The emotional elements that go to make up attachment are complex. To talk of 'love' alone is not enough and to talk of 'mother' alone is not enough either. Children require warmth in human response, sensitivity to their distress signals, and intensity in aspects of their interaction with others. These are provided by fathers and other family members, older siblings and other adult figures who may provide a regular part of the child's daily care-giving world. They are aspects of what mothers offer but they are not exclusive to mothers to provide. What inhibits successful attachment is apathy, the lack of response, and the failure of people in the child's immediate external world to be sensitive to his developmental needs. There is now good evidence that shared mothering and the dispersal of responsibility for the child's upbringing will not be harmful unless it is associated with inadequate interaction or too many discontinuities for the child. Children need not suffer from changing circumstances, whether in day nursery, with daily minder or shared care in the home, provided that the quality of care is maintained.

What stops adults attending to children's needs well enough?

Well, obviously disruptive, distorted interactions over time may stop adults attending to these areas for children. We can see that there are distortions of interaction in the areas I have mentioned—verbal, emotional, sexual interactions between parents both within the family and between parents and the outside world (for example recourse to drink, drugs or violence, or the persistent and severe failures caused by mental ill health in one of the parents).

These will not only create stressful interactions in the home at the time but will also provide distorted models for the future as the child grows up and makes choices both conscious and unconscious about what kind of person he will become. However, changes from the adult perspective leading to changes for the children may also come from life stress events for adults. Broad networks of problems that involve all sorts of losses, for example the loss of jobs through redundancy; the loss of country through immigration; the loss of intimate relationships; or loss of aspects of self through disability or long term illness. Recent research has shown that significant stressful events are perceived by adults as those that have a long term threat affecting the self, not crises of short duration. An event like immigration for example can either be seen as a rich opportunity for the development of new aspects of the individual, the family, or, where it is an experience of the loss of everything that is familiar, can seriously affect the quality of mental and emotional life. It is the way the event is perceived and experienced, not the event itself, that may determine whether the change is good or bad for family and child.

Ordinary life stress

Children also experience life stresses. They may have to face stressful change through ordinary life events, such as the birth of a sibling or entry into hospital. In a recent study by Judy Dunn[2] of the affect of the arrival of a new baby on the first born child, over half of children studied were found to become tearful and develop toileting problems following the birth of a sib, and a quarter developed sleeping difficulties. Whereas going into hospital on one occasion does not appear to be significantly associated with stress, a further admission can potentiate the stress experienced on the first occasion. But again the degree of stress displayed relates to the child's age, to the degree of separation from all to whom he is attached, and the way in which he is given an opportunity to make a new attachment in the hospital itself. These findings on children entering hospital may be equally appropriate for children in other circumstances, perhaps separated from their back home families in the West Indies. So I'd like to take this same fact—that it is the way that the event is perceived and experienced, and not the event itself, that may determine whether change is good or bad for family and child—and link it briefly to divorce.

134

Divorce and family dissolution: the child's experience

The way that the process of dissolution is handled is likely to affect the child's experience of the event. In the aftermath of divorce both parents will tend to be more inconsistent, less affectionate, and possibly lacking in control over the children. Mothers may become depressed and more self involved, more erratic in their child care, less supportive and more ineffectually authoritarian. Fathers have been found to be more indulgent and permissive but then increase in restrictiveness and the use of negative sanctions. Some recently published research by Wallerstein and Kelly[3] on the effects of divorce on children over a five year period made some useful distinctions between family structures related to good outcome and family structures related to poor outcome. Parenting can be maintained as a relatively conflict free area of behaviour even in the process of an unhappy marriage and separation. There is an important link in the child's capacity to cope and his understanding—his ability to make sense of the sequence of disruptive events within the family. Good outcome for the children was related to the extent to which divorce provided relief from previous rows; the extent to which appropriate developmental parenting was maintained within the home; the extent to which the child did not feel rejected in relation to the non-custodial parent and the regularity of that relationship if it was maintained over time. The fourth important fact was the availability of a supportive network for the child. While a good enough relationship with mother was important, an important contribution from this research was the emphasis on the maintenance of a two parent perspective following the divorce. The child continued to 'be aware of himself' in relation to both parents—'the two parent perspective remains significant despite legal and geographical separation and the passage of years.'

Poor outcome for children was related to the continuation of quarrelling equally or worse following divorce. A third of the children studied recognised intense bitterness between their parents at five year follow up. In these families adults often showed increased psychological instability and psychiatric illness, therefore the children had to deal with this as well as increased economic stress and bitterness between the parents. Secondly poor outcome was related to insufficiency of parenting and a lack of continuity of care where a relationship with living-in parents had deteriorated following the divorce. We can see here that the notions of distortion of interaction, or inadequacy of interaction and nurture, are as important as they are within marriage.

I am speaking again of these so we can separate the notions of what needs to be done and kept an eye on, on behalf of the child, from the particular form in which we are used, and I use 'used' in the sense of habituated, to thinking about how it should be done, i.e. the two parent family. The danger with habit is that it operates below the level of our conscious thinking processes, and it's therefore not available for examination, for modifying, and for change. But if we can keep the idea of what needs to be done more or less distinct from how it is done we are better able to help people believe that they have not done irretrievable damage to their children, and indeed to help make sure they don't do it. If we look at families in the process of separaton as part of a continuum which moves from two parent, to one parent, and then again into three or four parent family structures, or as in a recent family that I have been seeing a seven parent family structure, we can begin to look at how different structures need to develop different strengths and resources to deal with the hazards they are likely to have to face.

Divorce can be seen, as one American family therapist put it, as 'one of life's developmental dramas rich with possibilities for growth'. However, the shape of a single parent family with one adult having to meet the twin lines of authority and nurture in relation to the demands of children will have hazards that are different to those of a four or five parent family who are having to work out how the sharing of care is to be carried out without, for example, the attendant hazards of destructive competitiveness, or an over complex system of communication, signalling and rules for the children. Where these are unclear they will often hinder the successful psychological development of children. It is these difficulties that professionals need to help parents attend to.

Protective factors in the face of change

If we return again to the question of protective factors for children in changing circumstances, we return to questions of attachment and bonds, the development of self esteem in the child, and the development of coping skills. Several studies both of women who are mothers, and of children in families with distorted relationships between the parents, have shown the value of intimate, close and confiding relationships in times of stress. A good relationship with one parent is an important protective factor for children when the quality of interaction between the marital partners is severely distorted. Similarly a good relationship with an older sib or with an adult outside the family can protect the child from the effects of marital strife. The protective nature of bonds depends more on the quality, strength and security of the relationship than on the particular person with whom the relationship happens to be formed, and at times of disruption an alternative bond can do much to make better the stress experience.

In thinking then about change for children, we need to think about how to equip children to deal with it. The development of the child's own self-esteem, in combination with a development of coping skills, are both important. Adaptability and malleability are among the chief temperamental characteristics which protect children against psychiatric disorder, and context can do much to influence this development for children of all temperaments. Secure bonds need to be linked to developing opportunities for exploration and experiment. Children grow in self esteem as they master a variety of new situations and the attendant skills required to deal with them that they encounter as they grow up. The capacity to separate from parents and deal with things alone is centrally interrelated to security, but needs to be practised and developed as a skill to be mastered. I have suggested that children are capable of many kinds of change, but that an awareness of what they also need in the way of protection from stress or graded exposure to change will help them deal better, develop more adaptively, increase their flexibility, and increase the complexity of the situation with which they are equipped to cope. In the work I do with families I often use the image of the switchboard parent to differentiate the adult who acts as switchboard to the child, controlling them with signals but not helping them develop their own grasp of events, from the parent who helps the child to develop understanding of what is going on and of what his part in it is and can become. Where a child can use his thinking skills in a more objective way to decode what is going on, he will be able to master emotional stress more effectively and to generalise his learning to other situations. He will therefore grow up to manage a greater variety of changing aspects of family structure, changes in the roles of men and women, inter generation changes, changes between cultures, and changes within society as a whole.

References

1 Rutter M: 'Stress, Coping and Development: Some issues and some questions', Emmanuel Miller lecture: to be published in the *Journal of Child Psychology and Psychiatry*

2 Dunn, JF and Kendrick, C: 'The Arrival of a Sibling: Changes in patterns of interaction between mother and first born child, *Journal of Child Psychology and Psychiatry, 22.1,* 1-19, 1980

3 Wallerstein, J and Kelly, J: *Surviving the Breakup: How children and parents cope with divorce,* Grant McIntyre, 1980

137

Discussion

In many ways the discussion mirrored the speeches in that it centred on men, women and children. But another strand could be seen all the way through: how do men and women's roles relate to each other, and, bearing in mind the fundamental biological differences between the sexes, how do people interpret and work towards equality and sharing?

What emerged from the questions following Martin Richards' talk was that equality is not—and cannot be—a hard and fast equality of tasks between husband and wife. Only women can bear children, even if most fathers are present at the birth of their children nowadays. Breastfeeding, and the early closeness of mother and child, creates a bond which a father may find it hard to feel a part of. Many of the men Martin Richards talked to in the course of his work said having sole care of their child for at least 24 hours was very important in helping to build father-child relationships.

So sharing is something which must be worked out to the satisfaction of both partners but need not necessarily involve both in the same spheres of activity. There is no 'right' or 'wrong' way to achieve the notions of equality or sharing. There is no significant correlation of working wives and sharing, home participating husbands, and those couples who do share household matters and childcare may choose to fulfil their tasks together or turn and turn about.

Attitudes towards sharing and the importance of fathers to their families are only changing slowly. The responsibility for caring for elderly and dependent relatives still falls very heavily on women, and in 80 per cent of divorces it is still women who get the custody of their children. One bit of role stereotyping seems resistant to change in families; women continue to do the 'emotional housekeeping', which includes such things as remembering birthdays and anniversaries. Although some men enjoy the new opportunities they have for extending their home life with their families if they are unemployed, many find the consequent loss of work identity hard to cope with.

If you start by accepting that men should be encouraged to participate more in their families and to show their capacity for tenderness, then the question arises—how? One participant did in fact query whether men should not be prevented from encroaching into the realm of feelings which constitutes women's power—but there seemed to be tacit agreement from most that men should enter more into the private sphere of life, that men have feelings as parents and spouses but do not show or use them in the same way as women. It was suggested that it is patronising to talk of encouraging men to articulate their feelings. In groups run by this particular participant for engaged couples, men led the discussion. We must beware of creating a new stereotype of men as unable to express feelings.

What is needed is not change at an individual level, but change in thinking at a societal level which would in turn affect educational thinking. It was pointed out how from their earliest years boys are conditioned: by the kind of toys they are given; by being told not to cry; by being considered of secondary importance to girls where sex education and education in personal relationships are concerned; by being neglected as fathers by the relevant professionals when it comes to pre- and ante-natal care, childcare, parent-teacher contact and so on.

About three quarters of the participants were women. Pauline Crabbe interpreted this as the guilt, and feelings of responsibility for marriage and family, which is part of the social conditioning of women. But there was far more talk about men's roles, and it was a man who pointed out that the discussion of women's roles was very much in terms of how society has changed women, and not how women have changed and are coping with their own changing roles. It was also a man who drew attention to the changes in sexual attitudes—to the growing recognition of women's sexuality and needs which may be seen to threaten men.

In discussing how children cope with changing patterns of family life, including changing sex roles, the emphasis was on the relative merits of single, dual, and multiple parent families. Gill Gorell Barnes, in answer to a question which challenged the emphasis she put on 'attachment', reaffirmed the importance of this concept in the context of continuity of care. It does not need to be one person who brings up a child—several may be involved without any detriment to the child—but there must be continuity of care. For this reason, amongst others, the child in a one-parent family is not necessarily the most deprived child, as someone suggested.

One parent families need more resources outside the immediate family to help cope with children, but as long as it is clear what these resources are, children need not suffer. Martin Richards quoted research which suggests that the children of parents who divorce develop better psychologically if they remain in a one-parent family rather than joining a reconstituted family as a result of their parent's remarriage. Adults may be reluctant to look at the differences between a marriage and a remarriage, and the effects of that on the family structure.